THE
LEADER'S
2ND
TRAINING

THE
LEADER'S
2ND
TRAINING

FOR YOUR LIFE AND OUR WORLD

ARNOLD MINDELL, PhD

gatekeeper press

Columbus, Ohio

The Leader's 2nd Training: For Your Life and Our World

Published by Gatekeeper Press
2167 Stringtown Rd, Suite 109
Columbus, OH 43123-2989
www.GatekeeperPress.com

Back cover photo by Cathy Bernatt

ISBN (paperback): 9781642374322
eISBN: 9781642374315

Library of Congress Control Number: 2018968306

Printed in the United States of America

READERS' COMMENTS
about Arnold Mindell's

The LEADER'S 2nd TRAINING For Your Life and Our World

In *The Leader's 2nd Training*, Mindell persuasively proposes his grand idea of the Big Theory of Everything (the Big TOE), which includes not only Physics, but also Psychology, Spiritual experience, and Social Awareness. Based on the Big TOE, Mindell introduces the 2nd Training method, which consists of relaxing, fighting the enemy or bad thing, seeing ourselves from the enemy's viewpoint, and sensing the detached essence level where physics and psychology meet together. This new method will enable all 1st Trainings to work better. One of the key words of this book is that everyone is needed as a 2nd Training leader to facilitate conflict resolution worldwide.

—Prof. Takao Takahashi,
Emeritus Professor, Kumamoto University, Japan

Arnold Mindell describes how bringing in the dreaming is so crucial and desperately needed in everyday life and in politics, where the world of facts and consensus reality prevail. Linear solutions can be very helpful, but the greatest help comes from our deepest dreaming, from what Mindell calls our "essence level intelligence." More than who is right or wrong, we need this essence level ability to relate to each other.

—*Vassiliki Katrivanou,*
former member of the Greek Parliament and
Council of Europe (2012-2016),
and Processwork therapist

In this charming and insightful work Arny Mindell reveals how inner and outer worlds, physics and psychology share a deep connection to essence reality from which creative activity in the psyche as well as within nature originate. Knowing how to flow with, learn from and give voice to essence reality forms the core of the Leader's 2nd Training and is of great value to psychologists, physicists and anyone interested in the nature of their own reality as well as in that of the universe. But more than just theory Arny also provides exercises that help initiate the reader into their own experience of 2nd Training.

—*Dr. Jeff Raff,*
Jungian analyst and former president
of the C.G. Jung Institute of Colorado

Thanks

• • •

I FIRST WANT TO THANK Amy: that is, Dr. Amy Mindell. She is my wife and partner in all things. Her insights, artistic and musical contributions during my classes and the seminars we did together helped to create this book. Not only did she contribute in those ways, but she directed and organized the publishing of this book. Thanks, Amy, whom I sometimes call the Amy Mou Press!

Thanks, Susan Kocen, for your recording and wonderful work writing up class and seminar lectures! Your write-ups are basic to this book.

Thanks, Susan Newton, for your attention to detail and final editing! Also, thank you so much Linda Innes, for your in-depth review and initial editing of this work!

Also, thanks to you—dear several thousand people from around the world, who were present during my classes and our seminars (with Amy) these past few years. You helped me learn how to teach the 2nd Training!

Thanks to all my processwork colleagues and personal friends around the world for joining in and helping to create the process of learning and working together.

Finally, thanks to those world leaders who helped me realize how to adapt the 2nd Training to your world situations.

I could not have done this work, if it were not for each and every one of you!

And now, just as this book is being published, I want to thank Cathy Bernatt so much for creating and narrating the audio version of this book!

PREFACE
Big TOE for World Problems

("**TOE**" is a term borrowed from physics,
meaning a Theory Of Everything[1])

. . .

DEAR READER, YOU HAVE SURELY sensed, at one time or another, that to work best with personal and global conflicts in a sustainable manner, we need to understand the people, their groups, and organizations. We also must appreciate issues involved, including their identity, country, and all possible diversity issues: race, religion, sexual orientation, age, nationality, financial issues, history, health issues . . . and so forth.

We need to appreciate these issues and understand the nature of the world. The story of our earth includes astronomy, present and historical problems, diversity issues, psychology, bodywork, relationship work, economics, and spiritual experience. We must include these to try to resolve the problems of our planet!

Physicists such as Stephen Hawking and others have suggested that, to survive, our human race might need to leave our planet in 100 years.[2] (I discuss this problem in greater detail in the Appendix).

Until now, our psychology, social sciences, physics, and spiritual experience have been separated from one another. We need a new theory, a new idea, a *Big* Theory Of Everything or Big TOE. (John Ellis's "TOE" term was popularized by physicist Stephen Hawking[3]).

Until now, the TOE idea belonged to physics. However, my idea of a *Big* TOE includes not only physics, but also psychology, spirituality, and conflict methods. We need a Big TOE because we can no longer separate our personal psychology from conflict, history, spiritual experience, and the threatened future of our planet.

* * *

My own background includes my studies and work in the sciences, liberal arts, and psychologies. I learned a great deal from C. G. Jung, from my clients, and from Aboriginal peoples from Australia, Kenya, South Africa, India, South and North America, and around the world.

Marginalized peoples in the US and many other countries have expanded my understanding of diversity issues and encouraged working with social tensions to help our future planet. Thank you all, dear friends, for all your support.

Process-oriented psychology, also called Processwork, works with individual, large group, and organizational processes, in just about all states of consciousness. This work includes people's signals, dreams, and basic patterns seen in their earliest dreams. My *process concepts* developed from empirical observations, working with individuals and large organizations. This work is also connected to the ancient philosophical tradition of Chinese Taoism.

Processwork will always be in the process of development, as we learn more about working with the problems of our world. The practice of Processwork depends, of course, upon the nature of the individuals and groups involved. See the Bibliography[4] for more on the background of Processwork.

Dear psychological friends, get ready to think about other subjects. Physicists, be prepared to see our science used in new ways. Group facilitators and world leaders, be prepared for new ideas that may help our world.

To begin creating a Big TOE, I show how quantum theory, relativity, and newest ideas about the universe's dark energy are part of our universal psychological experience (involving self-reflection, and the bending of space and time). My goal is to show new and practical ways to work with yourself, relationships, organizations, and countries for more community and less violence.

In 1st Trainings, we learn leadership methods, sociology, medicine, physics, spiritual methods, processwork and/or other psychologies and spiritual traditions. But, to apply these methods and studies in tense and complex situations, we need a 2nd Training. 2nd Trainings involve process awareness and a sense of *FLOW* with the issues and peoples involved, during tense personal and world issues.

The 2nd Training appreciates that while your normal identity might not be able to handle some situations, 2nd Training awareness flows with just about any problem within yourself, in relationships, in government, and in our world.

Table of Contents

List of Illustrations

PART I

Quantum Aspects
of Consciousness

. . .

CHAPTER 1

The Big TOE and Quantum Woo

• • •

I COULD FEEL AND SEE the many people from around the world taking part in my recent class at the Processwork Institute of Portland, Oregon. In a way, dear reader, I feel as if you, too, were "on line" and in that class with me, as well.

I am writing and teaching, and at the same time learning with you. We all need to study how to help our world; how to help people work together to resolve the many ongoing conflicts.

In this first chapter, you will get a chance to experience how you can best lead on earth by sensing our universe.

1. Galaxy in the Universe

Universe? Why study that here, in the midst of all our social-historical problems? What does the universe have to do with conflict work? My answer is that thinking about the universe will give us an overview of ways to facilitate our little planet.

Let's begin by asking a big question. How did our known universe begin? We know there was a Big Bang, 13.8 billion years ago, but we don't know much about what made that Big Bang happen. How did our universe, our solar system, our earth—and all of us—get created?

I ask this question because, if we knew the answer, we might know how to help our many peoples on our little planet to survive, in our solar system, in this immense universe. I assure you in advance that having some knowledge about the physics of creation will help us develop new methods to get in contact with our deepest selves, work with body problems, and facilitate world events for the benefit of everyone.

Since I was 5 years old, I have wondered: how did we get here? What are we doing here, on this planet? How did our solar system arrive? Religions give us ideas, physics gives us other possibilities, and most of us try to forget these big questions.

2. Pope Francis & Stephen Hawking

For example, a few years ago, in the Vatican, when the physicist, Stephen Hawking, asked Pope Francis about what created this universe, what happened at the Big Bang, the Pope said, "Do not think about what happened before the Big Bang."[5]

Hawking said, "Why not?"

Was the Pope right to *not* think about the origin of the universe and to just believe in God? Was Hawking on the right track, wondering about what happened before, or at the moment of, the Big Bang? Each of us has our own feelings about that. Religions have answers, and science is looking for its answers, as well.

The question remains: "How did we get here?" I will approach such questions by valuing both deep psychological experiences, and real concrete scientific knowledge that we can measure.

For example, when I first studied psychology, dreams were crucial but how the body arrived on earth was not included in the dreaming process. *"If you have body problems, don't ask your therapist! Get real and see a medical doctor!"* we were told. We were good at separating things like body, mind, and world. However, psychology can't cut itself off from the body or the world, because what we think and dream are, in part, physical body experiences linked to worldly events.

For the same reason, physics must not be cut off from psychology or religion! People create and dream up the principles of physics, as well as the experiences of psychology and religion.

My point is that we need to unify psychology, physics, and spirituality. We need to bring them closer with a Big TOE: that is, a Big Theory Of Everything[6] to help our world. One of the reasons our present psychology and politics are not sufficiently helping our world is that we don't know enough about ourselves and our universe.

I remember the Nobel Prize-winning physicist, Richard Feynman. Today, he reminds me of the Pope. In his lectures on physics, Feynman said we should not think about the origins of the Schrödinger equation, which describes the essence of matter, the quantum mechanics of waves and particles. He said, "The equations just work." Feynman said, "Schrödinger's wave equation explanation just popped out of his head, he did not develop it. It works, that's all! . . . It's not possible to derive it from anything you know. It came out of the mind of Schrödinger."[7]

Feynman and the Pope basically said, "Nature is the way She is. Don't think further."

We must consider that if our dreams are connected to our thoughts and theories of the universe, then physics, religion, and psychology must somehow be connected.

ESSENCE LEVEL

When we ask where life and where our dreams come from, we are confronting similar basic questions. I call the level from which dreams come the "essence level". It's when you wonder about something, "sleep on it," and go to the deepest experience of dreaming and consciousness.

The essence level is the awareness level from which dreams pop up. I call the intelligence of that level our "processmind". You can feel or sense it when you relax: you may notice tiny thoughts and ideas popping up. I prefer "processmind" over terms such as the "unconscious" because of the remarkable, apparently nonlocal (or as Jung might say, "synchronistic") intelligence behind the processmind. Call that mind the Great Spirit, God, the Self or anything else, but experience it yourself to know it.

Here is how to feel this essence level whenever you need to. Just relax, let go, breathe in a pre-dream state, and let your body move . . . until images arise describing those movements. This is a simple way of noticing how new ideas, dreams, and sudden insights appear "out of nothing."

The level closer to everyday awareness or "dreamland" is where you have visual images or vague intuitions arising from that essence level. The essence level is like the quantum world of physics—you can barely sense or see it at first, yet it gives rise to dream images and thoughts, just as quantum events give rise to particle measurements.

THE BIG BANG

Let's now think about the beginning of the universe, the so-called "Big Bang". In a way, dreams are the result of little bangs. They can re-begin and re-orient our lives. Does the universe also create big bangs? That is, dreams that become realities? Perhaps . . .

In any case, we need a Big TOE, a big theory of everything. Processwork is one attempt—one of many future attempts—to create that Big TOE.

The universe is 13.8 billion years old. That is, 13.8 with 9 zeros. We know that there was a Big Bang but little about what made that Big Bang happen. Is our planet, solar system, galaxy, and world a dream, originating from that bang?

I'd compare the pre-dreaming state to the universe before the Big Bang. If you are in touch with your deepest self, you are in touch with the spontaneous creativity of our universe. In other words, our present universe came from a Big Bang—and our lives, thoughts, and dreams are similar.

QUANTUM THEORY AND SELF-REFLECTION

To study that pre-dreaming state, let's briefly look at quantum theory: the theory about the behavior of elementary waves and particles of matter. I know—everybody just loves quantum physics and you cannot wait to study it! Joking aside, quantum thinking is important.

The Quantum Wave equation describes the wave-like nature and behavior of tiny elementary particles. This wave equation is a bit like the dream patterns that organize the essence levels of our consciousness.

In physics, this equation describes particles before they are seen in terms of waves. I have written about this equation in detail in my book, *Quantum Mind.*[8]

The math of these patterns includes self-reflection. Because of that mathematical reflection, real measurable answers appear. For some unknown reason, physics says that this wave function self-reflects, to create reality. When the wave equation self-reflects, it produces real things we can measure.

The wave-like essence of matter seen in the wave equation self-reflects to get real results. Like processwork, we know if you relax and go deeply into your breathing and "waviness," the essence level self-reflects on itself and instead of a blurry, wavy feeling, you begin to notice dream-like events, which can help you to deal with reality.

Apparently, we must consider the possibility that inside you, me and the universe there is a tendency to self-reflect. When the wave function in quantum physics self-reflects, particles appear. When the essence level self-reflects in people, we may see images or dreams that help with everyday reality.

In the sense of the wave-like background in quantum theory, and the essence level in psychology, you, me and the universe are similar. Could it be, that at the essence level, who you are is timeless? The average person says, "NO! I am NOT timeless. I will one day get old. I must be careful, take vitamins, eat well, not get sick . . . !"

Yes, all that is true. The visible particle called "you" will die; but try to remain open to the possibility that the essence level part of you is not a particle or a thing—it is neither living nor dead, but is a wave-dreamy experience.

Think about it. Do you think you came from two people sleeping together? That is what everybody says. Maybe . . . but who we are is—at least in part—timeless! The material you're made of changes, but the essence of that material might have been here timelessly. You don't have to believe this; yet many people have talked about reincarnation, and quantum wave math suggests there is a tendency inside every human being for self-reflection and creation from the subtle essence level.

I recall the first time I worked with people in a coma, physicians asked, "What are you doing, talking to that person?" I said that I was just being open to possible communication above and beyond normal everyday consciousness. I discovered that if you work with the subtle signals of dying people, occasionally people come out of comatose states.[9]

In other words, even when we are dying, there is often (or may always be) some form of consciousness and re-creation trying to happen.

Reflection is part of quantum physics. Reflective consciousness and self-reflection are found in real people, events, and in the equations of quantum physics.

There is a part of us—the essence level, in psychology—that is also seen in the equations of quantum physics (the quantum wave equation), that reflects. We are usually not conscious of this level, and yet it tends to self-reflect in everything and everybody.

When you first wake up in the morning, if you don't get up too quickly, you will notice that one part of you starts thinking about the day, while another is still dreaming or reflects on dreams. Inside of you, something says, "What's going on, here? . . . Oh, a dream or deep feeling! Oooooh!" Then your everyday mind appears, and often marginalizes these experiences, unless you write them down.

Thus, we see this tendency to self-reflect, in both our psychology and in quantum physics. Nature may have an ingrained tendency to self-reflect. Even babies have it, as we all do—right through to the last moments of life . . . and maybe afterwards.

People who refuse this self-reflection over long periods of

time eventually get bored, ill, or depressed. What we call the flu is a sickness, but many diseases may be attempts to push you down to this wavy, blurry essence level. You need this level for your good health. We have an ingrained self-reflective brilliance. We need to drop out of consensus reality, or become tired, to open ourselves to experiencing the essence level. Burn-outs, depression, the flu, colds, feeling down, are good in one way: these events may be trying to get you deeper. Then, when you are down low enough, "it" often seems to bring you up, with new thoughts. Perhaps, this self-reflecting dream creator is a key to your health.

If we are all small parts that have this tendency to self-reflect—a group of people can also self-reflect. Therefore, a whole system of these small parts can reflect on a bigger system.

Is our planet, our solar system, our world, our universe, a living being in the sense of a self-reflecting being? My answer is . . . (I'll say it quietly) . . . *yes!* Why would I whisper it? Because the physicist in me says, "That is quantum 'woo'!"—meaning you are making something out of quantum physics that has not yet been proven. Therefore, I will say it quietly.

Let's remain open to the possibility that our universe has a tendency for consciousness and self-reflection seen in quantum equations, and therefore, it is potentially in all people, and all the things in our universe. In other words, reflection in physics is like wondering in psychology.

The essence level reflects on itself and creates a bang, in the sense of awakening us with a dream. Perhaps, in the beginning, before the big bang, the universe also went, "Wooo, wonder, self-reflection, and bang!" as it woke up.

We also yearn for a big bang when we get depressed or exhausted. We need a re-creation. That is, we need to re-experience ourselves reflecting, dreaming and—bang! . . . awakening.

DEEP DEMOCRACY AND THE BEGINNING OF THE UNIVERSE

Deep democracy is based upon an essence level that evolves into dreams at the dreamland level, as well as measurable events at the consensus reality level. Each level is, by nature, equally important. In fact, you cannot work in the world on big problems without some deep inner connection to that essence level. Otherwise, you tend to overwork and burn out.

Was the essence level, this quantum wave function, here before the universe began? I guess it was, prior to the beginning of the universe. It seems as if self-reflection is one way our universe began.

I am not alone in this thinking. I recall that Leibnitz, the theologian and mathematician, said many years ago that imaginary numbers—which today are basic to quantum physics' wave function—are halfway between existence and non-existence.[10]

The Aboriginal Australians refer to the essence level as Dreamtime, "a time out of time." You find this level also in the *Tibetan Book of the Dead,* in Judaism, and in Christianity—in the imagination that "God's spirit hovered over the form of lifeless matter, thereby making creation possible." In other words, belief in a god, whoever s/he was, is belief in a consciousness that brings things to life.

You don't have to be religious. I am simply saying that that the essence level and the quantum wave function share ideas with Aboriginal and modern religions. Perhaps we are beginning to intuit the connections between religion, processwork, physics, and the beginning of a Big TOE (Theory Of Everything).

Schrödinger, the developer of the quantum wave function idea, suspected that there must be another reality behind the wave function. He wondered if the waves of quantum waves were somehow real. David Bohm, another great physicist said, "isn't there a wave-like something in the background?" But no one has discovered that something yet.

In contrast to physics, religions and spiritual traditions like Buddhism suggest that we should *develop an empty mind!* That is very close to the essence level.

Even Feynman said, "Don't think about it, just calculate." The correct quantum wave equation just popped out of Schrödinger's head! He basically said, "Don't think about what you cannot prove."

So, physics says "no" to that which cannot be measured in consensus reality, in terms of space, time, and size. Similarly, some religious traditions say "no" to physics. In processwork, we try to bring physics and spiritual traditions closer together.

"Yes" to quantum physics and "yes" to empty-mind Buddhism. Quantum physics and the psychology of the essence level's tendency to self-reflect imply that self-reflection and creation are part of nature.

My basic point is that physics and psychology need each other, in order to understand themselves. We need to connect to creation and self-reflection to deal with the problems in our world.

Creation? It's part of our 2nd Training.

So, let's try the following exercise.

EXERCISE: RECREATE YOUR WORLD
(alone or in dyads)

1. Stand, or sit upright, at the edge of a chair. Relax and be BLURRY with a relaxed, mindless, essence level feeling. Note subtle body experiences, and relaxed sounds and movements arising. Notice when you or these subtle experiences tend to reflect on what they are.

2. Note how these subtle feelings or ideas eventually appear as dreamlike ideas or images. Remember, if you can, to feel the essence from which dreams appear. Also remember the dreamlike images.

3. With wonder, note any ideas + associations with those subtle essence feelings, and imagine using these associations and possible meanings to enrich your everyday life. Make a note about your learning.

4. Now feel those original subtle "WOO" tendencies as you return to everyday life. Staying close to this deep essence feeling is part of your 2nd Training.

Our friend Fukushima Roshi said we should meditate all the time, sense the essence level as *mu-shin*—no-mind—because that empty mind is beautiful. He liked to call that empty mind, "creative mind".

Different traditions and the sciences and psychology belong together.

We all need such deep essence feelings, 2nd Training creative connections, to work with ourselves and our conflicted world. We need access to the essence level, which connects our psychology to physics and spiritual traditions.

CHAPTER 2

2nd Training and Quantum Woo for Body Problems

. . .

To work sustainably in the world, we need to work sustainably with ourselves. So now, let's focus on how the 2nd Training and its essence level connection can help with body problems. This is perhaps the most powerful approach to symptoms I have come across. I have used it many times; also with people who were very ill.

ESSENCE LEVEL

Recall the discussion in the last chapter about the essence level, which we can experience as a kind of relaxed "emptiness." We correlated the essence level's rise into consciousness with self-reflection in quantum theory. I suggested that we should remain open to the possibility that our universe itself self-reflected, to become itself. Also recall that this quiet, powerful, reflective awareness tends to produce dream images and insights.

Zen Buddhism's "empty mind" is what I call the essence level.

In physics, this might be the phase before the universe began. Our friend, Fukushima Roshi, Chief Abbot of Tofuku-ji Sect in Kyoto called this level "empty mind" and "creative mind" because of its tendency to create dream images and new ideas.

As the experiences of this essence level/empty-creative mind arise in consciousness, I often call these early pre-dream experiences "flirts", because they momentarily attract your attention. When these flirts repeat in time, they become more easily seen, as they arise in the *dream-like* level—which means that they become images that you can hold onto; that you can call dreams or fantasies.

As these flirts come closer to your everyday consensus reality, you begin to wonder "what are these feelings, thoughts, or images?" If you focus on them, you discover that they are often offering new ways for you live in consensus reality, more consciously.

The 2nd Training is based upon the subtle and flowing experience of the origins of consciousness, and how the essence level and flirts emerge as dreams and ideas in consciousness creating a kind of psychological Big Bang. By Big Bang, I mean "Ah ha!" as new ideas arise from the essence level and dreaming. In other words, as I have suggested in the first chapter, the origins of consciousness are like the possible origin of the universe (based upon my quantum reflections in quantum theory).

If I made up a story about the universe, it would be something like this. Once upon a time, there was something amazing, which did not quite know itself . . . and it wondered: "Who am I? Hmmm . . . ." It noticed slight feelings arising and began to reflect on them. Then it noticed a big bang, or impulse to become reality. It awakened and realized, "I am the expanding universe!"

In any case, as I said in the last chapter, aspects of this *creation process* come from reflection in quantum theory and from process-oriented psychology's empirical view of how consciousness arises. (Remember, empirical means verifiable by observation or experience, rather than by theory). Self-reflection is apparently built into our universe, our essence level, and the so-called "psi function" of quantum physics.

NEAR-DEATH EXPERIENCE

Next, I apply these ideas to your body symptoms. As I have said, we see this essence-dream phenomenon in everyday life, and even in near-death experiences. For example, in a coma, people near the essence level often, or perhaps always, experience tiny flirts and even dreamlike experiences. I discuss this in detail in my book, *Coma: Key to Awakening*.

With awareness, you may be able to experience the essence level at night, even when you are snoring. We always seem to be active! There is no time off, as far as awareness and its levels are concerned.

The process of moving through levels of consciousness appears as phases. Levels are part of our consciousness process. Although I have written about these phases before[11], I will summarize them here.

The deepest level, the essence level, is a process phase I refer to as phase 4. In this level or phase, you notice vague, deep, detached feelings but have no images yet.

Phase 1 commonly occurs when you think, "Oh, here I am! Forget dreaming, I don't want to think about anything, I don't want any problems, leave me alone!" In this phase, we don't want more new thoughts or problems! That's phase 1: forget the other phases.

Amy and I were recently working on the tsunami and tidal waves' destruction in Fukushima, Japan. Thanks to Takeo Kiriyama for his work, there. We learned that many children were getting thyroid cancer from the remaining radiation. That terrible tsunami had occurred a few years earlier, but many Japanese had suffered a lot, just thinking about those terrible problems. They were thinking, "Leave us alone, we don't want to have to think about that painful event." They were in phase 1.

So, to do group processwork with those people and their government meant that we needed to acknowledge that many of them wanted to forget all the trouble. That forgetting is phase 1.

Phase 1 in organizational settings and worldwork is extremely important to appreciate. You can try to fight the tendency to avoid problems in phase 1. But people in phase 1 open more quickly if their need to avoid pain is appreciated. Only then, can they begin to deal with phase 2 problems.

In phase 2, the problem that you were ignoring—let's call it X—is back! Your inner critic and outer negative political figures are X figures, creating tension for many people in phase 2. Phase 2 is full of tension and conflict.

Phases 1 and 2 are what others would probably agree to as "consensus reality," relaxing and/or fighting.

In phase 3, the possibility of exploring that X problem, and/or role-switching becomes possible. The monsters you deal with in everyday reality often appear as dream figures at night. That implies that you are at least a bit like X. We need to face that X problem inside, as well as outside.

In phase 3, X is recognized as an aspect of yourself. Since you dream about X, there is the possibility of role-switching in phase 3, and discovering how you, too, are like that X. In psychological work and in worldwork, such role-switching can be crucial for relationships and solutions. Phase 3 is a dream-like phase, close to the essence level or phase 4.

Phase 4 is the essence experience within or behind the other phases and experiences. With awareness, you can go to this phase 4 essence level from any one of the other levels.

So, what we refer to normally as levels of consciousness are also typical phases that we all go through. We are not bound to fixed states of mind, but have phases, and are in constant process. Such phases are in the background of our inner and worldwork. *Quantum physics speaks about the wave function, which is, psychologically, a subtle phase 4 experience*—an essence level that cannot be measured. It is a wave-like pattern or essence, prior to dreaming and consensus reality. That's why I say the universe looks like it began with a consensus reality "bang" but it may have been preceded by a wave-like essence experience capable of self-reflection, before that Big Bang awakening in phases 1, 2, and 3.

The more I hear and see people in near-death experiences, the more I guess that our beginnings and endings may have cyclical phases, because few people dream about death itself as the end of all things.

Talking about quantum physics and the wave or "Ψ" function might seem like I'm talking in a new language you're not familiar with. But what physics calls that basic Ψ function is one aspect of a potentially self-reflecting universe that creates, and may recreate, its own realities.

In any case, *a Big TOE or a Big Theory of Everything* suggests that self-reflection, as in phase 3, is part of nature—and that it might have always been here, even before the Big Bang. Maybe there is even something of you that was here before you, something that self-reflected, to make you an observable physical form. You don't have to say "yes" to that, just be open to that possibility . . . in phase 4.

Can we prove that self-reflection was present at the beginning of the universe? As I have suggested, perhaps we are living inside a potentially conscious universe. I leave that open for you and the future to decide. My point is, in empty mind of phase 4, remain open to your own innate ability to self-reflect. Try to take your awareness as seriously as you can, and value it.

Now, comes a big world problem: the attitude that consensus reality is physically real and measurable, and therefore all the rest is "woo" and not measurable! This is like the average viewpoint— "forget your dreams! Wake up! Be real." This reminds me of a white teacher who told an Australian Aboriginal child, "Stop dreaming!" Yet, Aboriginal cultures taught us that dreaming and dreamtime are very important. Earlier cultures and belief systems did not marginalize the essence level. They would acknowledge all the phases: phases 1 and 2—and 3 and 4, as well.

Perhaps one of our biggest big world problems is our tendency to focus only on consensus reality in phase 1, and in phase 2: fighting. Today, most people ignore phase 3: role-switching, and phase 4: detaching, and therefore we marginalize our full potential, in conflict. We believe conflict means "get out there and fight" in phase 2. "Dreaming in phase

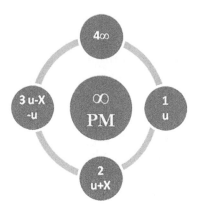

3. The phases and their relationship

3? Who needs that? To hell with that dreamlike junk! We have REAL problems! Let's get out and fight!" That's phase 2—which is a crucial phase, but not the only phase.

Phase 3 suggests that the things you hate are like you! Phase 3 is marginalized in politics, but not psychology. Everywhere in the "normal" world, people believe, "I am this. I am not the other, and I am *NOT* role-switching. No need to dream! This is the reality we have got to deal with!"

Fighting in phase 2 *is* important, but our relationship to the other side depends upon phase 3: role-switching; this is one of the keys to our worldwork. You can not only switch roles, but you can reflect on yourself from the other's viewpoint. This is a key to world problems.

In phase 2, you look at what is bothering you—X—and think, "let's get rid of it / go to the doctor / take an aspirin and shut up!" That makes sense sometimes, but remember to listen to that X! We will be doing that in the exercise, later.

Most of us are like the most rational doctors and one-sided politicians. We need phase 3 and phase 4.

Phase 3 shows us that we are not just talking about an X that bothers us. We are also thinking about another part of us, an X we don't know well.

In the 2nd Training, the essence level, deep, phase 4 state of mind is important. When we can sometimes feel that level, we can flow better with all the other phases.

The 2nd Training is based upon the openness of phase 4, and the way it can flow with all the other phases.

If, during a conflict, you can drop into the essence level—which at first has no images, only a sense of openness and quietness— you will flow better, which helps. If you can't do this, you will be surprised to find, at night, that you dream that you are like the other.

If you are in conflict, and you can really get into that relaxed phase 4, it helps you stay fluid between phase 1, 2, and 3. Sense phase 4 as much as possible in the 2nd Training. Phase 4 is fluidity, flow, and detachment, or what Fukushima Roshi called "empty mind, creative mind." He deliberately added the word "creative" to "empty mind." When you are in this phase 4 processmind state, you will be able to notice that new things pop up that you would hardly expect.

The 2nd Training is about experiencing phase 4 and its ability to relax in phase 1, fight in phase 2, dream and role-switch in phase 3, and detach in phase 4. No phase is right or wrong: all are needed to flow with nature.

I recall a powerful example of phase 4 and deepest dreaming when Amy and I were in Australia. One of the Aboriginal elders said to us, as we were walking down the street in Adelaide, "Look there! What do you see in the city? Do you see the city?"

I said, "Yes."

He said, "Look there, at the river. What do you see?"

I said, "Traffic, pollution, smoke, the people."

He said, "You are not looking closely enough. Don't you see the Aboriginal people still there, playing and working by the river?"

It made me realize that my perspectives at that time were mainly phase 1 and phase 2. That is, consensus reality—and I was missing the dreaming.

He said that today's modern city would not be there, if those Aboriginal people were not there in the background, in dreamtime. Without them, the city would not have survived.

In other words, learn about the 2nd Training. Learn to stay close to phase 4, which is the essence-like background to what most cultures call reality today.

Symptom Work

Let's apply the 2nd Training phase awareness to body symptoms. Before beginning our symptom work, I want to give an example of the FOUR phases, which will make it easier to apply the 2nd Training to symptom work.

From Wikipedia, we read that Isaac Newton, an English mathematician, astronomer, theologian, and physicist, is widely recognized as one of the most influential scientists of all time. He was a key figure in the scientific revolution, "one of the great founders of modern physics." Here is the story of how he discovered gravity.

He was thinking about gravity, according to a story, when

he was hit by an apple that dropped from a tree. Then, he realized there was something he called *gravity* pulling that apple downwards. Phase 2 awakened him to gravity, so to speak.

4. Notice, Learn + Grow

In the second picture, Isaac Newton looks happier as he eats the apple that hit him. He integrated the apple in phase 3. It became a part of him, so to speak.

So, whatever is catching your attention, "eat" it. Try it to integrate it into your life, as well as working with it in consensus reality. Do this especially with body symptoms.

Fight the "apple," that is, the thing bothering you, in phase 2. Try to integrate or eat it in phase 3. Whatever you see, reflect on it, be it, and integrate it.

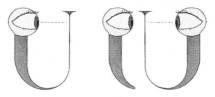

**5. Left: John Wheeler's Universe reflects;
Right: Universe reflects its self-reflection,
aware of awareness in Dreams, Dreambody + CR**

In phase 1 and phase 2, forget and fight what is bothering you. If it is a body symptom, try medicine to fight it. But medicine usually represses phase 3: the fact that you are the X thing or energy or experience bothering you.

The Dreambody idea, on the other hand, is that *you are your dreams, and you are like the body feelings* that bother you. So, feel your symptoms and ask yourself how you *are* that symptom energy. This Dreambody work begins to integrate Aboriginal thinking.

Fanny Brewster, an African American Jungian analyst, recently wrote, "I believe that Mindell's approach to Dreamwork, with its emphasis on body healing, mirrors the African system of healing's inclusiveness of body and mind in the process."[12]

This reminds me of experiences Amy and I had in the East Coast of Kenya with the Giriama tribe, whom we met in 1986. Although Amy and I were not yet married, they said to us, "We see a married couple. We really like you. We are going to baptize you. And now, you are African!"

"How can we be African? We have white skin!"

"You are African!" they said.

They helped me understand that many aspects of phase 3 in Dreambody work and role-switching in worldwork are multi-cultural. We "are" the other.

Let me give an example of Dreambody work. I had a cold recently—so I took Vitamin C: I fought the cold (phase 2), and I recuperated in a few days.

But since I was a little tired afterwards, I realized that I needed that fatigue, and went with it. The X was tiredness that felt like an ocean carrying me. So, in phase 3, I looked at myself through that ocean's eye and I saw something quite amazing. From the ocean's viewpoint, I, Arny, looked very linear and structured. That helped me to change and flow more.

See yourself from the viewpoint of X, of your symptom, and you will find a key to your psychology and good health. I had a cold and I was tired for a week afterwards. I was doing a lot of things and was rigidly tense in phase 2. From the viewpoint of phase 3, I realized that I was not flowing enough. My problem was that the ocean was arising to make me more fluid. So, I switched roles, as in phase 3, and entered phase 4—becoming the ocean that flows.

Medicine is important to "fight" problems in 2, but it is not the whole story. Medicine is typical Newtonian physics, which is push and pull. It is phase 2—"fight it"—an important aspect, but not the whole process.

Practice role-switching with symptom energies. Remember also to look at yourself from the viewpoint of the symptom, discover its viewpoint, and bring that into life.

In worldwork, we must do the same as in symptom work; that is see yourself from the viewpoint of the X. Like relationship problems, your body symptom is something to experience, act out, and explore.

Instead of the word "phase," let's use the *# sign for phase.*
2nd Training involves:

#1: relaxing with the symptom,

#2: fighting it with medicine or alternative medicine,

#3: becoming the thing bothering you and looking at ourselves through its mind,

#4: flowing through all this with detachment.

JESUS AND THE MEDIUM

If you pick up information in your 2nd Training, and move through the phases, amazing things can happen.

This reminds me of a woman I met years ago, who said she

heard Jesus telling her to go to Los Angeles airport. Then Jesus told her to ask people for money to buy a ticket. Then, Jesus said, "Buy a ticket to Zurich, Switzerland." She landed in Zurich, got out of the airplane, and Jesus said, "Open the phone book and call that number."

She called me, where I was working at the time. I was in the middle of my practice and did not have time, but she said, "Jesus told me to call you."

Because I love different kinds of clients, I said, "Come on over."

She was wonderful—especially in following the #4 essence level she called Jesus. She, or Jesus, told me all sorts of things. She said, "I saw you do something in your bed under your covers at night that was not quite in conjunction with the person you are living with at this time."

I said, "Jesus has a lot of insight!"

She was a year or two ahead of my getting divorced. She could see everything.

Twenty years later, this woman appeared at our front door. Amy opened the door, and the woman said, "You must be Amy!" and threw herself into her arms. Amy had never met her before. That woman was very direct!

She said, "I followed an eagle to find your house."

Amy said, "OK!"

Then, when she said her name, Amy recognized it from me. She called me, "Arny! She is here!"

We had tea and had an incredible conversation. She said to me, "What you are doing will be on the stairs of the White House and it will influence our educational systems. But it will take years."

Then, she flew out of the house again, and that was the last we saw of her!

She was showing her experience of phase 4, being open to the universe, and following whatever it wanted. If she had known more about the other phases, she would have been a great 2nd Training teacher.

Now, let's work on our bodies. Remember, in a way, the body is the container for dreams, a Dreambody we may have marginalized.

EXERCISE: 2ND TRAINING BODYWORK: EAT YOUR SYMPTOM AND LOOK THROUGH ITS EYES

1. Choose your worst body problem. It can be an imaginary symptom you fear but may not have fully experienced. Or it can be a "real" symptom. In any case, call it *Symptom X*. In a way, it is like Newton's apple that hits you on the head: it bothers you. Do you know what the symptom is due to? For example, is it due to being nervous? Are there medical ways of helping with that problem?

2. Ask: What is the most troublesome X energy like, in that symptom? Describe it in words. Act out the X energy. Have you noticed if, and how, that X energy is often in the background, trying to arise and catch your attention in dreams, body symptoms, and in everyday life?

3. Now, relax in #4, drop down inside, and feel the essence level. Feel the essence of that symptom before it is something. As you notice essence sensations, let images of those sensations arise by themselves. Just stay with the sensation, notice dream-like images, feelings, and thoughts arising.

4. Be *that essence and symptom energy and let it form an image*. Act out the image and be it. Now in #3, look at

27

yourself through the symptom energy's eyes. Yes, SEE your ordinary SELF THROUGH ITS EYES, until it gives you a tip about life. Then, imagine living that tip.

5. Now, imagine using that tip to help yourself and to relate to others. Don't keep insights to yourself; your symptoms don't belong to you, they belong to the environment. Please tell anybody who is interested about your symptom message. Sketch X's essence-experience tip and make notes.

If body symptoms belong to all of us, it should be possible to create body symptom "activism." For example, a group of people in a breast cancer center could work on breast cancer together, even if they don't have the symptom itself. The essence of the symptom is nonlocal. I have always said that so-called "extreme" states belong to the city: they are not only an illness or problem. The same thing is true about body symptoms. If you are not shy, and you are in a situation where you can share your symptom image and energy, please do it.

Remember: what we call symptoms come from essence experiences. At first, the symptom seems like a problem—until you see it in your 2nd Training as a problem in #2. Then, in #3 as a way you can better understand who you are, and in #4, as a potential gift for yourself and the world. Your 2nd Training in bodywork, moving fluidly through the phases, may create relief, as well as solutions for your body problems and our world.

CHAPTER 3

Lucid Living and Possible Reasons We Are Here

. . .

2ND TRAININGS ARE BASED ON flowing with the deepest phase 4, or rather, #4 experiences, as well as with the other levels and phases, with:

#1, just enjoying life

#2, fighting and defending what you feel is right

#3, switching roles with the parts and people in life that disturb you—and

#4, realizing detachment is a phase, too, not a law!

The 2nd Training will help us all to follow our deepest dreams and essence level in all we do.

This 2nd Training will eventually help our world to work better together. Such a training is based upon a Big TOE that interconnects our sciences, psychologies, medicine, and spiritual traditions.

Recall the reflective tendency inside the equations of quantum mechanics that have no known reason for being there except that quantum theory works, as far as physicists are concerned. When considering the possible beginnings of the universe, I have suggested that the dreamlike reflective ability seen in those equations might be characteristic of matter everywhere. I have suggested that the so-called material world contains the seeds of consciousness. Aboriginal and Native peoples have been saying this since the beginning of time, so I am just supporting and moving with that important idea forwards. In other words, our world and universe are self-reflective.

This suggests that all so-called material things are potentially self-reflective. Therefore, don't just kick your car, or a chair! Instead, please think of material things as potentially self-reflective. You cannot lose anything with this attitude: it might actually help our world.

In the last chapter, we talked about getting to the essence of symptoms, and learning to live and move from the essence: from the inside, out. Look at yourself from the viewpoint of your symptoms—that is, phase 3, which is part of your 2nd Training!

Remember, your symptoms may be a key to health and wellness. Pills are fine, but we need to also listen to the body, as we do our dreams. Why don't we do that? What do you think?

6. Crinkled Dark Paper

I love modern medicine. I take a pill if I need it, but that's only the beginning of the story. Remember, symptom work has phases, like all processes. There is an essence area, distant from consciousness. We notice the origin of symptoms as tiny flirt-like things, trying to catch our attention in #1. Then, in dreamland, where dreams appear, symptoms appear as dream images, and in consensus reality, symptoms become "real."

Remember in phase 3, self-reflection is possible, and you can, and need to, look through the eyes of the symptom at yourself. So, instead of talking further about symptoms, I want to do a quick experiment.

EXPERIMENT: Here is a piece of dark paper. Take a look, and let yourself begin to see something in the paper.

Maybe you can imagine something portrayed by that paper. Let your fantasy flow. Can you see a little bit of a face in there, somewhere?

Now, imagine the face is looking at you—and just ask yourself to go into that face here and look at yourself through its eyes. Let the face give you a tip, or some advice.

What tip does this face give you? What message did you get?

Here are some comments I received from students who did this experiment:

- I saw a dolphin face—not a human face. It said, "be more playful."

- I got, "Stop being so serious!"—the same thing!

- I saw an upside-down cave bear with the cross of the medicine wheel in his mouth, and it said, "Listen to all directions and speak from all space."

Wow! This experiment helps you understand why it is important to pick up flirts. Many people say, "I don't dream," or

31

"I have no dreams." My point is that *everyone has a great potential for dreaming in #4 and reflecting with flirts in #3.*

In other words*, your dreams are always with you.* Processwork suggests a paradigm shift. You *always* have a dream with you. You are never alone: you always have some wisdom figure with you.

Yes, you might sometimes feel alone, but you are never alone. Even if you are in hospital, your dreaming is always with you, giving you tips about what the next step ought to be. Whatever flirts with you, whatever catches your attention, briefly—hold it, and look at yourself from its viewpoint. It is something you need in the moment. Whether you must work in front of a group or on a hot political situation, or you are working with individuals, remember your dreaming mind.

You may usually identify with phases 1 or 2 in everyday consciousness, but phase 3 flirts are always trying to reach your conscious mind. Use them reflectively. *Seeing through the eyes of what is trying to catch your attention can be a key to understanding yourself, to relationship work, and worldwork.* Update your awareness. Remember, notice and flow with all possible levels and their phases.

Dreams in dreamland are in #3, bordering on the essence level of #4. To really work well with a dream, you need to look at yourself from the viewpoint of the dream figures. That is not the whole of dreamwork: you also need dialogue (our #3), as Jung pointed out years ago, in a method he called "active imagination."

The 2nd Training attitude understands that whatever or whoever catches your attention *tends to see you, as well.* Anything that catches your attention is also looking at you.

You don't have to use this solely with symptoms. Don't wait until you get a cold or don't feel well to meditate on what is flirting with you. See yourself through the viewpoint of all that catches your attention.

One of the world's big problems is not only a lack of dialogue between world leaders, but there is too little dialogue between you and yourself! We lead our lives and work with conflict and political issues in #2, but the dreaming aspect of dialogue is often missing—looking at yourself through the eyes of the opponent, at least temporarily. You still need to fight and sometimes even overcome the other person. But if you let in #3 reflection, your 2nd Training will help whatever you are doing to be more sustainable.

A core 2nd Training message is that Flow Wisdom is always with you. You are never alone. That is important, because sometimes you can feel pretty much alone, but you are *never* alone!

Our spiritual teacher and friend, the Roshi, would have called the #4 aspect of the 2nd Training *empty mind and creative mind.* Processwork's essence level is empty, and it gives rise to creative mind as part of the overall flow of the 2nd Training.

7. Haida Houses+Totem Poles 1878.
(Wikimedia Commons; Photo by G. M. Dawson)

I remember the wonderful Haida people, with whom we worked some years ago, who live on the Canadian northwest coast. One of them told us, "We don't need electronic radios when we go out to sea to fish."

I said, "How do you know when the weather is getting bad? You can get into trouble without radios."

"No," they said. "We look back in the direction of our totem pole and *it* tells us what the weather report is."

There is nothing wrong with radio electronics, but it is just not the whole story. Flirts and messages come from the spirit of those Totem poles; from nature.

DREAMS

So, when essence experiences reach the dream image level, we say, "Oh, a dream! I had a dream last night," and wonder about that dream. Remember its essence level origins. Remember, #4 might appear as sleepiness. It's not just that you are sleepy and need to go to sleep—you need to be, and go, deeper. You may get sleepy during the day not only because you need a nap, but because you need to dream.

You may feel like coming out with force in #2, especially when you are working for world change. However, don't forget your deeper levels and phases of awareness in public. This leads me to ask . . .

DOES LIFE HAVE A MEANING?

Everybody has their own viewpoint about this. Maybe one of life's meanings is to be aware of the origins and flow of consciousness. Maybe the meaning of some people's lives is to follow the 2nd Training process, being with #4, and flowing with the other phases, to help oneself and others.

Among the many meanings of life, one might be to notice your awareness process and to help others interested in it. Notice and appreciate the amazing human being that you are. You have these various flowing levels of awareness. Support them, relax, wrestle with problems, reflect, and become really creative. Whether you do this alone, one-on-one, or in large groups, your 2nd Training enables you and others to be most helpful and create relationships where tensions existed before.

The Gods

Spiritual traditions often imply that there is spirit behind life. Many spiritual traditions make rules: "You must behave in consensus reality this way—and not that way." They move into #2 and fight some parts and some people.

Empirically, the Great Spirit behind #4 and the various god images are the powers behind the essence level trying to catch your attention in #3.

One of the things I learned during my own Jungian analysis with Barbara Hannah and Franz Riklin was to follow the moment. (See the pictures below.)

8. Left: Franz Riklin; Right: Barbara Hannah

Barbara Hannah would say, "If you want an analysis of dreams, go downstairs to von Franz!"

I said, "But I am coming to see you!"

"I don't analyze dreams."

I said, "Oh? What do you do?" She would do all sorts of amazing, miraculous, intuitive things—which were as good as, if not better than, ordinary dreamwork.

I went to see Hannah once and said, "I notice that cigarette in the ashtray has lipstick on it. Who did it belong to?"

"WHY are YOU looking at that cigarette?" She was picking up on what I now call pre-dream flirts.

"I don't know!"

She said, "I have a sense you are interested in women!"

That was about a year before I realized it was time to find another partner. She was pretty good with pre-dream flirts! That cigarette with lipstick interested me. Even though she was trained in dream analysis, she was better with flirts.

My favorite of all my analysts was Franz Riklin, the president of the Jung Institute in Zurich at that time. He rarely analyzed any of my dreams. He was always very spontaneous and burst out with all sorts of things. I learned and grew so much from his unconventional ways.

My recommendation is to notice people and things that catch your attention—and *look at yourself through their eyes!* If I'd done that at the time, I would have looked at myself from the viewpoint of the lipstick on that cigarette and said, "Hey! There are a lot of good things waiting for you out there!" I would have awakened earlier to relationship work.

NONLOCALITY

Things that pop and bubble up are *often nonlocally connected to outer situations.* As in quantum physics, changes in one particle in a system can be connected, at a distance, to another particle in that system. Flirts that pop up *may be* connected to other flirts happening to others connected at a distance.

Keep your mind open to that. I don't have proof of it, but the people at the Institute of Noetic Sciences in San Francisco are conducting research to prove what I am saying.

FLIRTS AND DEATH

In a "Psychology Today" article on Near Death Experiences,[13] it said that, near their brain-death, 10-11% of people dream that life is *going on* and that *People often dream there is light* at the end of the tunnel. This was supposed to be the most popular vision seen. Light. That sounds like the wisdom of #4 is always present, even when we are supposed to be dying.

Why do people who are dying see light at the end of a dark tunnel? Perhaps we are nonlocal, *timeless, awareness patterns, connected to past and future events.* Let us explore that now.

EXERCISE: EXPLORE YOUR PRESENT AWARENESS PATTERN (alone or in dyads)

What is the biggest personal, relationship, or world issue that bothers you most? Call it X.

1. Relax, breathe, and quietly experience your sentient #4 essence level—your pre-image, pre-dream, and pre-consensus reality experience. Notice how that sentient experience moves you, makes sounds and repetitive movements, and experiences.

2. Track the images and feelings of that experience emerging into dream figures in dreamland.

3. Let your everyday consensus reality-self wonder, and associate potential meanings to these arising images, sounds, ideas, and feelings.

4. If possible, let these experiences give your ordinary self some tips.

5. Use the experiences and insights to work with that troublesome personal X or world X energy or issue bothering you.

6. Now switch roles: be that X, and *see yourself through X's eyes. What does it say about you?*

7. Make notes about what your insights might imply about the meaning of your life just now.

Let's explore this by describing some work I did in a class, with a student, K.

Arny: Before we begin, I wanted to ask you to guess: Why are you here? Do you have any sense? It can change from day to day. Do you have any sense in this moment of what are you doing here? Today?

K: I think I am here to dream. I exist by a very fine sequence of chance and luck. My father came through the Holocaust. His whole family was murdered. I always feel that. He always said that he only survived by sheer luck, by taking a right where someone else took a left, by going up one staircase instead of another, getting onto one train instead of a second. So, I always feel the miracle of being alive.

Arny: Yes, it is a miracle to be alive. I am sorry for everyone who suffered so much—terrible. And . . . what is the biggest personal, relationship, or world issue that bothers you the most? You don't have to say, if it is too personal.

K: The biggest world issue is what we are doing to our planet, what our greed is doing to our finite resource. It is terrible . . . our greediness, our unconsciousness. We are abusing the planet, the people, the indigenous ways.

Arny: OK, now relax if you can. Relax a little. Breathe so much, you can feel a bit altered.

K: [goes inside, bends knees a little, breathes with open mouth]

Arny: Take those breaths, and settle into a relaxed state, a kind of pre-dreaming relaxing.

K: [big breaths]

Arny: Good. Now you are getting down to the subtle sentient essence level. OK. Notice now, how it moves you and makes sounds; makes repetitive motions.

K: [continues breaths, with body trembling]

Arny: That is it. Let it shake and move you . . . and follow your repetitive motions . . . experiences. Track those feelings, and maybe dream images will eventually appear.

K: [breaths become louder, body moves, hands rise]

Arny: That is it. I see you shaking, hands reaching out like that, sounds arising. Maybe potential meanings will appear.

K: [inhaling, exhaling big loud sounds of breath. Giggles] I feel breath, and tides, and I feel the seasons. I feel the whole— going inward, then outward, then returning. [. . . more breathing, arms move in and out]

Arny: And while you experience that, see if you can remember K in her normal state of being, so you can give her a tip about something. Take a look at K, down there . . .

K: I don't have language yet . . . [whispers] . . . Remember this! Remember this!

Arny: What should we remember?

K: [big breath] K, remember that you are infinite, and tiny, minuscule and . . . [big exhalation] and don't be so human! Don't be so separate from me! [starts to cry—big breaths again]

Arny: (as K) I am too separate from you? I should just let things come and go?

K: *You are only here for such a short time span, so don't be separate from me.* [big breath again, in and out] *Remember the bigger picture.* As my astrobiologist friend says, in 200 or 300 years, we will be good again. And then I asked him, what about the 200 or 300 years? And he said, yes, that will be pretty bad, but in 200 or 300 years fossil fuels will be gone, the population will have become smaller, and the next thing will happen.

Arny: But if I act as the normal K, I must say, "I am all uptight about that."

K: *Too bad!* [laughs] *Do your best. Live simply, tread gently . . . and remember me . . . and enjoy "me" . . . You suffer a lot . . . detach from your suffering. Because I know, K, that you suffer. So, definitely, detach from that, more often . . . and remember me. It is in your breath, not too far away.*

Arny: (Still playing K) You are right in my breath? (Now playing the breath-spirit) Remember this [shows breathing]. You, K, are smiling. You are closer to it now. Even when you get uptight about this, even when you are nervous . . . [breaths]

K: There you are! There I am. *There we are!*

Arny: Yes, yes, there we are. Switching roles, going back and forth. What might all of this imply about why you are here?

K: [pauses] . . . I am shy. I think *I am here to learn to love. I think I was born from something so hateful, I think I was born to learn to love well.*

Arny: Mmm . . . and how will this breathing essence experience help you to learn how to love?

K: Because I forget, and love is right here in my breath. In the breath . . . [to the group] Can we all do it, together? [Group joins her, big breaths, big sounds]

Arny: Yes, and I will add one more thing about why you are here. You are here to teach detached and flowing love, like you just did with the group. Thank you!

K: Thank you, Arny.

Another student, A: I wanted to thank K—and share a part of my personal myth. In the Yoruba culture in Brazil, there is the *Candomblé* and Odisha belief system. And you, K, just embodied Iansa[14] the wind goddess. Candomblé is an Afro animistic belief system. Everything has a soul: even a chair, a rock . . . and Iansa's color is red. So, it was really amazing to see you there, in red, bending the wind around you and creating that goddess.

Arny: K's lucidity and work with phases 3 and 4 allowed her to embody that wind goddess. Thank you, K, and everyone.

If there is anything you need to remember from this chapter, remember to pick up flirts and see yourself through their eyes. Remember the 2nd Training, which is the experience of #4 and #3, and the motions and dreaming that create an amazing, spiritual, realistic, and informative dance—and the reason for your existence.

9. Wind Goddess, IANSA Yoruba Culture

PART II

Einstein's Relativity +
Don Juan's Shamanism

• • •

CHAPTER 4

Deep Democracy, Relativity, and Shamanism

. . .

WE STUDIED REFLECTION IN THE first chapters. It appears that reflection in the math of quantum theory and reflection in the psychology of human awareness are linked and universal. Perhaps we live in a self-reflecting universe. Since Freud and Jung, we notice reflecting tendencies in our dreams, and we notice reflection in processwork, with flirts briefly catching our attention.

To work with those flirts, relax, whenever possible, into the essence level, #4, and reflect on what catches your attention in #3. See yourself through the eyes of what flirts with you. This flirt work is a core element of the 2nd Training.

From the 2nd Training viewpoint, a major world problem is not just the "evil" ones out there in the world—the so-called "bad" or X people, organizations, and situations—but also, our own rejection of #3's self-reflection. We need to feel into X's world and reflect on ourselves from its viewpoint. World problems are not just due to "bad" X problems and people, but also to our lack of phase consciousness.

Recall:

- phase 1: relaxing,

- phase 2: fighting the X,

- phase 3: feeling into and seeing ourselves from X's viewpoint and

- phase 4: sensing the detached essence level that allows us to flow best in the 2nd Training with all phases.

Now, let's study awareness in terms of the physics of light. Light supports our visual awareness ability. We will then study the effect of what I shall call *emotional mass and gravity* on our light, our awareness.

GRAVITY

See Einstein[15] on the right. He explained that what Newton called gravity results from massive objects bending space in the universe—or, more accurately, bending space-time geometry.

Like the psychological inner spaces of different people, gravity bends the space of different galaxies or worlds. Einstein showed that the speed of light is constant in all galaxies, even

10. Einstein

though the spaces in those galaxies are different and curved by the various masses of celestial material.

In psychology, instead of huge masses distorting the spaces of different galaxies, we speak of huge emotions bending our "light": that is, our awareness and thinking. Yet, in psychology—as in physics—regardless of the amount of gravity or emotions present that are bending and curving our worlds, *awareness* is always present. Awareness is like light itself, a constant in all spaces.

Before Einstein discovered relativity, physicists believed that time could be separated from space. In his special relativity theory, however, Einstein showed that time and space are fused together into a single 4-dimensional "space-time."

To help understand all this, see the diagrams below. On the left, you see a space-time galaxy or world without much gravity (or, in psychology, without much emotional mass). There, space-time is unbent, or just about flat, so we can see straight ahead.

But (see the middle picture)—with lots of big planets—or psychologically, with huge emotions—we can't see straight anymore, since our world (space-time) has been curved.

Yet, on the right, the speed of light—or what I am calling our awareness—is always constant and present.

Thanks to Einstein for showing us that whether our worlds are twisted by huge gravitational forces (or big emotional problems), the speed of light (or awareness) is always the same.

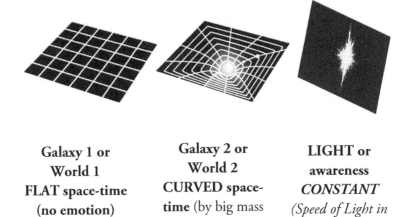

| Galaxy 1 or World 1 FLAT space-time (no emotion) | Galaxy 2 or World 2 CURVED space-time (by big mass + energy) | LIGHT or awareness CONSTANT (*Speed of Light in both worlds*) |

11. Spacetime and Light Diagrams for 2 Different Worlds

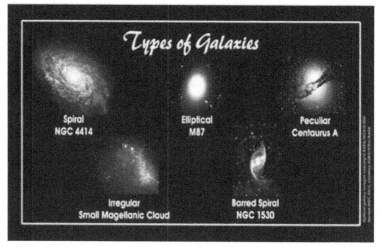

12. Types of galaxies

There is no single, fixed frame of time + space reference in our universe. There is only the constant speed of light, or its symbolic analogy in psychology: namely, our potential for awareness.

This unchanging and detached LIGHT, or what I am calling "our awareness potential," will help us to get along with one another, even those living in very different worlds, and to realize that there is no single right framework for all worlds. Only light or awareness is constant.

Relativity can help us with conflict work. Relativity suggests that the unchanging speed of light is independent of great masses and energies present. This is analogous to the unchanging light of our awareness, which is independent of emotions.

Say you and your opponent, or u + X, have very different energies and live in very different worlds. Our potentially unchanging awareness makes it possible for opponents to be potentially aware, and to understand one another.

Within ourselves, we are sometimes aware of altered states of consciousness, especially during emotional times. Nevertheless, there is almost always a dreaming ability: a constant speed of light in us that can illuminate and makes things potentially understandable—not only in our own, but in other worlds. We are all, each in our own world or galaxy, potentially gifted with light—that is, awareness.

In physics, the speed of light (in a vacuum) remains the same everywhere—in all basic and different (or inertial) reference frames—like in our solar system, and other galaxies. Because light maintains the same speed in all systems, it is an understandable symbol of awareness.

Symbolically, light, like consciousness, helps us to understand. That is why we sometimes say, "Oh! S/he sees the light!" This implies that they understand. "Seeing the light" means that we might disagree, but we are still able to understand and relate to people who think differently from us.

In principle, we can potentially relate to everyone—even in massively conflicted u + X relationships and worlds—regardless of the world or galaxy our friends or opponents live in. I personally know this is possible, because of my work with people in conflict areas, and in extreme states of consciousness.[16]

This awareness ability reminds me of the Biblical figure of awareness—Joseph, and his coat of many colors (Genesis, 37.3). He always had light with him. Even when people were against him, he could read into their worlds. (See the image of Joseph holding all worlds, that is, all stars and galaxies).

13. Joseph and his coat of many colors.
(Thanks to pinterest.co.uk)

EXAMPLES OF SPACE AND TIME IN EVERYDAY LANGUAGE

When you are near certain people with heavy moods, they can make you feel that something powerful is repelling or squeezing your sense of space and time.

Let's say you are a young student in school and the teacher demands that you get your work done perfectly and quickly! If you get too close to this teacher and you are not doing well in school, space gets really tense, and time feels reduced. You think, "Oh, my god! I had better do things quickly!" Space and time seem to shrink with the demand, "Do it now!" Suddenly there is almost no space and too little time!

There are many space and time terms in the English language. For example, "I am spaced out," "it's spacious," or "it feels cramped in here!" are expressions of different kinds of spaces.

Or remember time idioms such as "Time flies," "Stop wasting time," "Time is running out," "Take your time," or "We have all the time in the world," and so forth.

Terms such as "feeling uptight" refer to the sense of being cramped in both space and time. Sometimes, we experience time and space clashing. Think of a boss saying, "Hurry up and get your stuff done!" when the worker feels s/he has "all the time in the world."

See Salvador Dali's painting of time melting, "The Persistence of Memory."[17] See the clocks melting: lots of timelessness and spaciousness, all in one.

Dali painted this shortly after Einstein came out with relativity, and some people thought that this picture symbolized Einstein's theory of relativity which showed that gravity can bend space and time.

14. Salvador Dali, "The Persistence of Memory"
(Thanks Wikipedia)

OK. Now, that's enough theory; or too much, for people interested mainly in psychology. Let's practice some inner work.

EXPERIMENT WITH SPACE AND TIME

This inner work is simple and will show you more about space and time. You will need a piece of paper and something to write with.

- Make a square on your paper. Take a moment, and relax your neck and your head . . . and just breathe, for a time.

- When you are ready, just feel, or sense, or imagine what happens in the space of that square when you are relaxed. What do you feel or imagine is happening in, or coming out of, that square in the moment?

- Let your imagination come spontaneously, and when you are ready, just draw that on the paper, in some simple way.

- Now, when you are ready, sitting or standing— move, act out, and become whatever you found in that square: whatever you just drew. Use your arms, your whole body. Just for a minute, become and express the thing you just drew in that square.

- What kind of time does that experience have? Is it very slow? Or sporadic? Quick? Erratic? Elongated? Rhythmic? What is space like? Is it endless? Is it cramped?

- When you have a sense of these times and spaces, make a note on your paper about what you learned. Your art speaks in part about space and time, and may suggest new experiences that update your normal everyday identity.

- Look at yourself through your drawing's eyes and give yourself a tip. Imagine living that dreamlike space-time world experience.

LIGHT, SPACE, TIME, AND REFLECTION IN CONFLICT WORK

Now, let's think about world problems. As I have said before, one reason for world conflicts is that we usually suffer from one-sidedly thinking that our world is the only one. We don't have contact with the larger universe. Most of us were not taught in elementary school to use our light and *illuminate*—that is, to use our awareness light to work on conflict. We all need to illuminate the times and spaces of all people in all worlds.

Recall that in psychology, as in Einstein's relativity, space can be tight or expansive, depending upon the emotions (and massiveness, or masses) involved. Remember the idea that although we may live in different worlds, we all share the same speed of light, and the same basic ability to reflect. Not only do we find these potential abilities in the reflecting potential found in quantum theory, but also in the idea that there is one constant speed of light in the universe.

The idea of a speed of light being always the same, in all galaxies, regardless of where you are, is important for our world. For you, space might be straight—but for somebody else it can be curved, so don't expect it to be straight for everyone. This doesn't mean there is anything wrong with you—or with them.

If all this disturbs you, you are normal and conventional. You may not have learned about relativity and used your 2nd Training ability to relate to their cramped, painful, or detached spaces and times.

Remember, there is no one fixed reference frame in our universe. *All worlds are normal.* In mainstream groups, we create consensus realities that fit many people, but our views of normal times and spaces often divide us academically, psychologically, racially, physically, and medically, from others.

So, remember that the constant speed of light in all worlds symbolizes your potential awareness and gives you the ability to shamanize, or dream, in conflict.

Cognitive aspects of worldwork can be taught: cognitive aspects like roles and changing roles, double signals. All these things, we can talk about.

But if you want to work on world problems and survive, and if you want to work in the middle of tense situations with individuals or organizations without burning out, you need a 2nd Training. The 2nd Training means having access to your *constant speed of light: that is, your ability to see into your own and other people's spaces, all of which are normal.* You can disagree with people, but all worlds are, in a sense, normal.

Fear of death often occurs during social and world tensions. Death is terrible; but the threat of death does not just suggest that you protect yourself, it can also suggest a shift into phase 4, into the deepest timeless experience.

If you work in tense, political situations, or with organizational tensions, you might sometimes think it is too much for you. "Oh, my god! This might kill me!"

Politicians are often worried about death. It can be a real threat, but it is always a suggestion to protect yourself, as well as to let go of your everyday experience and experience phase 4: the relaxed space and time experience. This can make life easier. The more you are polarized, stuck in your own world and sense of time and space, the more death becomes a background threat that makes you nervous. But the idea of death can help you to relax and enter phase 4, to see clearly into the world of others.

The 2nd Training experience is based upon this occasional experience of phase 4 while seeing into other worlds.

PROCESSWORK, CASTANEDA, AND THE DEATHWALK

I have always been thankful to Carlos Castaneda,[18] and to his sorcerer, Don Juan, with whom he studied. Don Juan taught that *"Death is your greatest ally."*

In Castaneda's books, Don Juan speaks about surviving the deathwalk. The deathwalk occurs when people you work with, or friends, reject you for some reason; perhaps if you are doing something new that irritates them. In any case, if your friends or others in the world around you no longer like you, your deathwalk begins.

Don Juan says that sorcerers were able to survive the deathwalk and no one could harm them. Their health was not impaired. He does not say how that happened, but I am going to make a recommendation how to do it, now.

I use a new term, *lifewalk* instead of deathwalk, because conflict does not have to be a death event. When your normal way of doing things and fighting no longer works, your lifewalk begins. By lifewalk, I mean using #4 relaxed space and time fluidity. Remember, your #4 light or essence level experience is an unchanging awareness (like the speed of light) in all possible galaxies or worlds.

From the viewpoint of the #4 lifewalk, extreme tension is an opportunity to use your 2nd Training. Imagine facing a tense situation in the world, or everyday life, and literally letting go as much as possible.

With your 2nd Training, you can drop out, temporarily, into the dreamworld—into this lifewalk state. You will be able to read into the time and space of the *other* person so that you can interact with them with nearly total understanding, as well as appreciating your own side. You are not just in your world, separate, criticizing or stating your wisdom to the other person. The point is to value your normal state of being, and then *in the 2nd Training to let go, open up, and flow through all phases with the other(s).*

LIFEWALK WITH A WORLD X FIGURE (OR A WORLDWORK RELATIONSHIP ISSUE)

I give an example in the following exercise that Amy did, using President Trump, who might be a popular figure for this exercise, for many. In any case, you choose any world or social issue to focus on. When Amy was doing the movement part of the following exercise, she ended up with her arms flung open, and her chest opened. She was completely open—and she used that sense of openness to read into the time and space of Trump. This was an amazing shamanistic experience. The point is to read into the time and space of the X and their world.

I will give another example. Once, many years ago, in Switzerland, I was working with one of the most important people in the political world. World issues were coming up—and I did not know what to do. Then my dog, Cleopatra, who had been lying on the ground, got up, walked behind the other person's chair and . . . vomited! What a messy situation! She threw up, in back of this famous person.

I did not yet know about #4 energy at that time. But I realized that he and I needed to let go of his aloof space and time—and get down and help clean up our messy world.

It was clear what the next step was, so I said, "I know you may not be used to cleaning up other people's messes on the floor, but I will take one rag and you take the other rag and let's clean up that dog mess together." We cleaned up the vomit. My dog, Cleopatra, was very helpful in showing me and the other person how to relax out of our positions, work together and with people, and clean up a mess.

If I had been able to find my #4, maybe Cleo would not have thrown up. In any case, I said, "Come on, let's join the general population and clean up together."

Now in this exercise, the person doing the exercise will choose and work on a world or social issue that is important and disturbs them. We are going to ask you to then find the X energy of that most disturbing person or group. You will make a sound and a motion for that energy.

Then we will ask you to "die"—that is, to drop out of your consensus reality mind. Let go—and notice your breathing and body motions. (You don't have to throw up!) Reflect on your body motions and allow spontaneous images and motions to arise. Those experiences can help you to "light up" and feel into the spaces and times of the other person's problems and their X energy, and look back at yourself through their eyes.

If you work with someone else, your partner can play that X person and you can then explore interacting with them.

EXERCISE: LIFEWALK FOR A WORLDWORK RELATIONSHIP ISSUE (alone or in dyads)

1. Choose and describe one world or social issue that disturbs you emotionally. Make a sound that expresses the energy of an X person or group in that issue that upsets you, your health, or your life. Feel that X energy, then make a motion that expresses it and sketch it on paper. *(Partner, pay attention so you can play the X later.)*

2. Now, sit on the edge of your chair and imagine "dying." That is, relax and let go completely and notice your breathing and spontaneous body motions until they begin to repeat. Note your feelings and images of these experiences. Take your time. Sketch and name these experiences. Let's call these experiences your lifewalk.

3. Now, stand if you can, and recall and re-feel your lifewalk. Feel and move it. Breathe it, and when ready, use this experience to *light up* and feel into X's sense of space. It may be very different from your present feeling. Now, feel into and sense X's sense of time. What is their time like? Make notes. Then ask yourself, how have you experienced X's time and/or space in yourself, in some way? Now, look through X's eyes at yourself. How do you look through X's eyes? Make a note about insights.

4. Now, look at and feel your lifewalk sketch and insights again and imagine using these to relate and deal with X and the situation. Make notes. Finally, imagine X (*OR partner play X*) and practice, or imagine practicing, the lifewalk insights that you just experienced in the relationship. Speak for X about how you look through their eyes, and with your 2nd Training lifewalk and #4 experience, relate to X.

Here is the example Amy and I worked on with a student, F.

Amy: Is there a world or social issue you would choose that disturbs you, emotionally?

F: Yes, I have been struggling since the Trump election. His explosive X quality disturbs me. Everywhere he goes, he explodes. I cannot keep up with my many reactions. In the world, he is blowing things up. That's what X feels like for me. [shows her hand going up] . . . *boom!* It's like grenades! *Boom!*

Amy: Could you make a sketch of that energy and give it a name?

F: [draws a little grenade, then makes lines exploding out] *Blowing things up. There's shrapnel hitting on the side. Things get hurt.* Boom!

Amy: OK. We will put that picture to the side just for a minute and get to your lifewalk. We are going to imagine you are dying. By that, I mean just taking time to relax.

F: OK. I will sit down on the floor. [sits on the floor]

Amy: OK, relax and try to let go as completely as possible and notice your breathing.

F: [wiggles, slumps forward and backward, till undulations occur]

Amy: Notice repetitive movements that happen . . . and repetitive feelings and images that may come along with that experience.

F: I am not Jewish, but I feel I am *davening* (praying). There is a giving in and a coming back. There is a great broken heart.

Amy: Follow those feelings and movements

F: [more davening then, arms outstretched, reaching out as she goes forwards] I am not quite sure what this is . . . It is something about letting go and give it away . . .

Amy: Let go and give it away.

F: I can give away [leans forward] . . . When I am here, with my arms wide open, I can hold everything. But I feel I cannot stay . . . I am not allowed to do this, to go inside, to gather and rest. . . . Yes . . . I have not had enough of this inward time. How do you do this when there is so much happening?

Arny: Yes. How can you do this [shows relaxation, with head in hands] when there is so much happening?

F: [laughs]

Arny: Going back inside is almost not allowed.

F: That is not allowed—I think I feel I have to be out all the time.

Amy: Because there is so much demand and so much need.

F: Yes, I am not really allowed to do this . . . going inside. It makes me feel stingy.

Amy: While you are standing, feel that process. Get in touch with going out, and then, deeply, going in.

F: [repeats the same movement—moving from the ground, reaching up high]

Amy: Feel it, move it, breathe it, have it. And as you are doing that, see if that experience allows you to feel into the space and time of Trump's X energy, that Boom!

F: [makes motions; then a long, exaggerated, "Booooooo-ooo— ommmm!" (Moves around the room) Boooo-ooo-ooomm! It is kind of fun!! (Whole group joins in)

Amy: And do you know this in yourself, somehow?

F: Yes. It's like, "Blow the shit up! It's freeing! *I am so sick of being good*!!" YES! Destroy stuff! My process blows stuff up! Stop being so sensitive about other people! Be rude to them, when needed!

Amy: And then, with that knowledge, look through the *X-boom-Trump energy* eyes, back at yourself. How do you look, through its eyes?

F: There is a smile—it's like there's a common energy. Yes.

Arny: [Acting out the boom] Who wants to be sweet all the time? Boooomm!!

Amy: Now, imagine him looking back with that Booming energy, at F?

F: At ordinary F, or *Booming F*?

Amy: Whichever you like.

F: Well, if he is looking back at ordinary F, she is tiny. *But if he is looking back at Boom-F there is the whole, powerful women's march, right there! There is a matching energy!* Oh, I see! I must sometimes leave that "regular" F. Then, there is a matching Boom energy with the X. Boom! [goes forwards towards Amy's chest, with her chest!]

Amy: [laughs] With those insights, can you imagine how best to relate to him?

F: Well, one of the answers, at least for me, right now, *is for me not to be so fucking good!* [Her chest bumps Arny again!]

Arny: Wow! If I was Trump, I suddenly realized she is the more powerful one. She has got power.

F: And listen—there are a lot of us!

Arny: Millions of you!

F: And there is a match. *He is being met!*

Amy: Can you imagine how you would do that? How you would bring your lifewalk bumping-into relationship? That coming out and going in. How you would bring that, if you had to relate to him or go further with him?

Arny: [acting like Trump] *Here I am! I know what is right! Follow me!*

F: [bumps him again!] PAY ATTENTION! Meet me! Don't be off, tweeting your bullshit! Meet me back! Pay attention! You are not paying attention!

Arny [as Trump] I know what is right!

F: NO, YOU DON'T!!!! No single one of us knows what is right. It must be a burden, doing it like this! I think you are burdened and stuck!

Arny: [runs away]

F: Come back! Maybe we could talk?

Arny: [shrugs] Would you like to be Vice-President?

F: NOOO! But there is something good about getting attention! Being met! Thank you!!!

Arny: [as Trump, explaining to the seminar participants] She shut me up. I wanted to boom at her, but she met me, stomach to stomach.

So, F showed that for her, 2nd Training detachment meant following her basic nature, her phase 4 process; not just being quiet and inward. Her phase 4 light allowed her to see through X's eyes and realize that she had been too quiet. This light reduced the darkness and enabled change to happen. #4 was a death of the ordinary self and becoming so open-minded that her whole true self could come out with a booming dance. #4 is not just a quiet *Om* meditation, but light and consciousness enabling a detached and more creative communication.

Remember the deathwalk, or rather, lifewalk, in personal and worldly relationships. Let go, find #4 and light. With that light, enter X's galaxy; see yourself through the X's eyes. Then return to yourself and relate to X according to your lifewalk insights. F was surprised with what happened. She appeared to be quiet, and then—boomed! You, too, might be surprised at the changes that can happen to you and to relationships.

CHAPTER 5

Your Lifewalk in Group Process with an Enemy

• • •

As you learn to work with conflict using your light and ability to read into all worlds, and as you learn to see yourself through the eyes of others, you will probably be more at ease and more effective in tense conflict situations. You might even have more interest in helping our world. The lifewalk and your light will connect you to your most creative mind.

Without your phase 4 experience, you and everybody else seems stiff, frozen, or one-sided in conflict. If you want to facilitate conflicts, you need your deathwalk, or what I have been calling the lifewalk. Remember light. When you are in the #4 dance experience, you are, at least temporarily, enlightened—in the sense of being able to see more clearly and illuminate the other's world and their altered states. Your detached experience will direct you in dealing with existing tensions.

Remember, light does not change its speed as it moves through other galaxies. Our ability to understand others and ourselves, in any state of consciousness, is a potential ability in everyone.

This brings processwork and physics closer to spiritual traditions. Spiritual traditions also speak about light. People around the world identify their goddesses and gods in terms of light. Perhaps your phase 4 light experience will appear as a goddess, god, or guru in your dreams.

Let's now practice this constant light for when you need it in the midst of small group tension. You can practice it in small groups working on world or social issues.

I am aware that in tense situations, it's hard to facilitate and easy to lose track. That is why I want to stay in touch with the lifewalk light in the next exercise.

EXERCISE: LIFEWALK FOR SMALL GROUP WORLD PROCESS

3-4 people are best for learning. Take about 60 minutes.

1. *(10 minutes)* Spin the pen to choose a Guide who will lead everyone through the exercise, and also, participate. *Briefly* introduce yourselves. Then each *briefly* mention a world topic that interests you. (*Guide, write these topics down*). Then Guide reads each issue, one after the other, asking everyone to make a sound showing their interest in working on that topic. Choose the topic that has the most sound/emotion. Person whose issue was chosen: say a bit more about the topic and describe the most difficult X person/group in that issue, for you.

2. *(10 minutes)* Inner work *(led by Guide):* Each imagine the most difficult X in the topic for you. (Could be the same or different from the one just mentioned.) Make a gesture for the X's energy and sketch this energy on a piece of paper.

3. Now, sitting on the edge of your chair or standing, each should create a deathwalk/ lifewalk sketch by letting go and "dying." That is, dropping out, breathing deeply, and waiting for repetitive movements, feelings, and images to emerge. Relax and let your body sketch this lifewalk experience. Feel and be moved by your lifewalk light sketch and use it to illuminate and explore X's sense of space and time. How have you experienced their time and space? Now look at and feel your lifewalk sketch experience again and let it advise you how to deal with, and relate best to, X. Imagine doing that, now. Make a note, to remember your insights.

4. *(30 minutes)* Small Group Process *(Guide, read all of this, first)*: Person whose issue was chosen, name a central u + X polarity in that world situation issue, for you.

5. *Now you and others* begin to play X + u—and dialogue together. If and when needed, bring in ghost roles (of people and events). Any person/thing mentioned that is not present in the group is a ghost role; so, please, someone enact that role as necessary. Explore switching roles, and so forth.

6. When all are ready, whether they were needed or not, each should recall their own lifewalk experience and advice *to relate best,* while continuing dialogue. In any case, stop at relaxed or cool spots to review what cooled things off.

7. *(10 minutes)* All together, each note your learning and share this with others when ready.

Part of process-oriented group process or worldwork is to represent all sides and let yourself flow, change roles, and see through the eyes of each role. You might notice double signals: someone physically doing something that seems to contradict what they are saying. For example, someone frowning or grinding teeth while telling someone, "I really like you," is a double signal. Encourage people to note such signals and bring them into the group relationship processes.

Notice cool or hot spots. A cool spot means a momentary resolution, or a cooler quiet spot. A hot spot is an intense, "woof!" moment. If either of those happens, see if you can slow down, hold the moment, and explore those cool or hot incidents.

If you don't slow down at cool spots, you can miss the cooling off factor—which might be a potential key to the group process issue.

Above all, try to remember the #4 essence level and your lifewalk experience. Use that experience and your insights in dealing with X.

The central idea of the exercise is to get in touch with your lifewalk and use it to deal with the most difficult roles in the situation. Remember, your lifewalk's spontaneous motions are your light. You have the light and ability you need to read into the various spaces and times of the other—the X.

Einstein said, "The only thing I want to know is what's in God's mind. The rest are details." Maybe, now, we can tell Einstein, "Wiggling and finding light is on God's mind!"

Before you go to bed at night, don't forget to do your life wiggle-walk, the dance of the processmind. If you want to know what you will dream before you dream it, get up and let your body move around in a leisurely way, and from that, you may notice some important, dream-like experience emerging. As it arises, make a note of it; then, if you dream at night, check out in the morning if your wiggle experience was somehow in your dream.

Don't say you don't dream, because you can always wiggle. You don't have to go to sleep at night, to dream.

EXAMPLES OF EXPERIENCES FROM THE SMALL GROUP WORK THAT FOLLOWED

One group worked on the possibility of nuclear war with North Korea—and the outcome! They discovered: "Women Power! Women are going to solve it. The women will rise up and stop this nonsense and basically, they will change the countries from the grassroots upwards!"

Another group worked on the Dakota Pipeline in the USA: the problem of environmental degradation on Native American property. One said, "I have been with the Sioux for the last 20 years, so this small group work was very insightful. The first discovery I made was those who want to explore that pipeline project are powerful and potentially intelligent. I never thought about it this way, I thought these business and government leaders were simply stupid and ignorant and 'we'—the activists—were right!

"Then, in our process, as a government leader, I looked at the environmental activists. Their points seemed unintelligent, and the others were so mature and direct—responsible! The people who want to explore and exploit the earth have a lot of power! The hippie activists are fluff in comparison. That was one insight.

"Another insight was, as humankind grows bigger, we will go through stages of development. We will understand we cannot destroy everything. However, to get what we need, a new and next stage of environmental awareness and development must occur.

"The third insight was that we need to wait for the generation building these anti-environmental things to die. The young people, the younger generations, will be more capable and open minded.

For example, my mother who lived in a village and worked on the earth was like Trump. She thinks the earth is for people to use. But my daughter does not think that way. She will be less self-centered and open to all. Humankind will grow."

Another seminar participant said: "I want to talk about how my lifewalk affected the group process. My lifewalk experience was like a mudslide. We were working on how to deal with unchecked political power. In the group process, I just fell to my knees. That felt so good, because I don't often facilitate and because I don't know how to bridge gaps. The thing I realized—my irrational tip—my lifewalk tip—was about going deeper with communication. This was kind of magic, for me. I had to really trust magic, even if I cannot understand it in the moment. I had to trust the lifewalk, the thing that comes out of the dreaming. It will light up and show the way!"

Yes. We are always looking for linear solutions to things, which is good; but most of the time, the solutions come from deeper dreaming and the essence-level light. Please practice the 2nd Training, by using your light to illuminate your viewpoint and to see through the eyes of others.

CHAPTER 6

Beethoven's God and Einstein's Light

. . .

WE HAVE BEEN FOCUSING ON integrating light, a central concept from physics, into psychology. Everyone has light that can help show the way. Light is a *constant* in the physical universe, with its many diverse galaxies and worlds. Light seems to be a constant, a dependable awareness that is always present in all human beings, throughout their lives, from the beginning until the last moments of life. That light or awareness is there during good times, and during difficult times—when dealing with your own and others' angry altered states of consciousness. It might even be present at death.

In principle, light—as it appears in our dreaming ability—can illuminate not only your own world, but the worlds of others in conflict with you. Light helps not only to illuminate, but also enables us to feel and see into the worlds of those people or groups that are difficult for us.

Therefore, 2nd Training facilitation means, in part, getting in touch with that light. That is, feeling into the times and spaces of people, to relate more deeply with them. In a way, light is a shamanistic ability—mirrored in the stories about Don Juan, and in biblical images.

Remember Joseph and his coat of many colors, and how he was able to feel into the worlds of the people who were very cruel to him? Remember how his light connected to people who were even against him, enabling him to resolve problems? Also, recall your own lifewalk, another experience of deeply experiencing your own light, and how that may have helped you to relate to troublesome X energies and people.

15. Joseph
(Thanks to
pinterest.co.uk)

Now, let's find this light in sound and music. Music adds to the experience of the 2nd Training. Many musicians, scientists, and mystics have suggested that, in the beginning, the cosmos was filled not only with light, but also with vibrations and sounds. Scientists have shown that the origin of the universe was accompanied by sounds.[19] You can hear that sound suggestion, even in the Big Bang concept.

Many healers and shamans—and maybe some of you reading this book—use sound and light to enter altered states, to work on problems. The healers we were with in Mombasa did their amazing healing with us when their deep experiences transformed into chanting, creating a soundscape—a sound-environment—to support their healing methods.

In that Mombasa tribe, healing one person enabled the healing of all. Healing one person helped the whole village. In shamanistic or witch-doctor traditions, you don't have a problem independently of your village. You cannot have a problem without the world around you also suffering in some way from something similar.

Those wonderful people started the healing ceremony with us, and when they were finished with us, they started healing their own people, as well. We thought, at first, "Hey! This is our healing!" But they started to go around to everybody—and it was a beautiful, amazing experience.

SOUNDS OF THE SOUL

In a film about Beethoven, he talks about music as *the language of God*—"The vibrations in the air are the breath of God speaking to a woman's or man's soul. Music is the language of God."[20]

Altered states of consciousness allow us to see the light and hear the music emerging from the essence level that we can use for inner work and conflict work. The essence level appears in the film *Copying Beethoven*[21] when a woman who was Beethoven's music note-maker said to him, "Oh, you are telling me I must find the silence in myself so that I can hear the music."

Beethoven responds, "Yes, silence is the key: the silence between the notes, and when that silence envelopes you, then, your soul can sing."

The essence level's light can express itself through many channels: in movement, in sound, as visions, and so forth.

So, let's get in touch with Beethoven's key: silence. Then, we can perhaps hear the sounds and the vibrations that arise. We will let those sounds help us to feel into the spaces and times of our most difficult problems (as we did with light).

When in need or when nervous, Amy finds herself going to her piano or guitar, and when she starts to play and sing, it is like light to her, because she has the sense of getting to the essence level. She feels that no matter what she must face and no matter how terrified she is, music helps her feel that she will find the way and make something good out of the situation.

SOUND AND LIGHT FOR WORLD ISSUES

In summary, let me remind you of the light in your altered states of consciousness, the constant speed of light in all galaxies and in all worlds different from your own. Your own most detached awareness can access that light, and work with just about anything, anywhere. That is important, because if you work in extremely tense situations or tense galaxies, in relationships or on world issues, things are easier with light—and with its expression in sounds and music.

We will use your 2nd Training light experience and Einstein's relativity to get along with others. From now on, instead of saying, "Those other people are impossible to deal with!" I hope you say, "Let me try to read into them."

We need YOU to facilitate our world and read into others. We need you to integrate processmind ideas and god symbols, sounds, and tunes.

I ask the scientist part of me, "Why did the human race need to dream up god and goddess images? Why?" There is no one answer, of course. One possible answer is that we lose contact with that dream light intelligence and it is easier to remember when it belongs to a divine image.

"God is Light." For example, in the Bible, in John 1:5, we find: "This is the message we had heard from him, and announced to you, that God is light, and in him there is no darkness."

In the Quran, we read, *"Allah* is the *light* of the heavens and the earth. The example of His *light* is like a niche, within which is a lamp . . . and *Allah* is knowing of all things."[22]

One of the Lakota-Sioux prayers says, *"Grandfather, Great Spirit, fill us with light, give us the strength to understand and the eyes to see, teach us to walk the soft earth as relatives to everything that lives."*[23]

#4—LIGHT AND SOUND

Your deep #4 essence experiences manifest not only as light, but also as music. Beethoven called the vibrations in the air the breath of something divine: the breath of God speaking to people. To understand all this, just think of a song. What song comes to your mind, right now? The sounds and music you hear are important for you in a given moment and may have special messages you need. Try to hear a song, especially when you are in a tense situation.

Like all spontaneous dreaming insights, music belongs to your 2nd Training. It can help to detach you from #2, to go more deeply into things. Remember that 1st Training is following signals, noticing ghost roles, switching roles and so forth. *The 2nd Training is about finding, at least momentarily, a phase 4 experience through body movements, sounds or other means to facilitate yourself,* relationships, and world situations. Your 2nd Training will allow you to do this in a temporarily relaxed manner.

LIGHT IN SOUND

Choose a central problem to work with. We are going to imagine an X figure and energy. Then we will let space move us and while breathing and moving we are going to ask you *to listen and sense and hear any vibrations and sounds that come to you as you begin to move.* We are going to let them unfold. They might be a hum, a melody or a song you already know, or something totally new and weird. Then you will use that movement and sound experience to feel into the spaces and times of that X energy. Finally, your partner will play the X figure and you will try to use your light or sound insights to deal with that relationship.

Exercise: How Vibrations and Sounds Help Inner Conflict (alone or in dyads)

1. Choose a difficult, long-term inner problem and make a note about it.

2. In consensus reality, note any helpful energies and any destructive or hurtful X energies or viewpoints associated with that problem. Feel the worst X energy, act it out; imagine it as a figure and play it out. What is its world like? That is, what are its spaces and times like? Make notes.

3. Stand if you can, and relax your mind and body. Breathe, move carefully and let your relaxed phase 4 movement experience arise. And as you breathe and move, let space, vibrations, sounds or music in the air move you, and sing through you.

4. While moving, feeling, hearing and singing, recall the X energy. Use this musical experience to explore X's space and time. Then role-switch from u to X and use the sounds and feelings to understand X.

5. Now, with that musical insight, try to relate to X, and to X's time and space world. Take your time and make notes about any insights. Imagine integrating these insights and what they imply for your inner problem. Make notes.

Let's see now how this looks in H's situation.

Amy: Do you have a difficult long-term problem you would like to work on?

H: I often fear dipping into depression, a state of inertia. There have been times in my life when I have really gone into it for long periods of time, and it always feels like it is lurking.

Amy: Are there any helpful energies or things you use that help that lurking depression?

H: Yeah, a sense of lightness or energy. I listen to a lot of silly 80s music.

Amy: Can you think of an 80s song, in the moment? What kind of feeling does that music have?

H: The music I hear is very staccato. It has a lot of attitude and energy. [shows a movement, hand flips, hips move]

Amy: Good. Let's think about a possible hurtful energy associated with that sense of depression. What troublesome X energy makes depression difficult?

H: There is sense of frozenness . . . I am getting pictures of permafrost, super-condensed and cold—and atoms are not moving.

Amy: Feel it and see if you can imagine a figure or person of some sort. Who or what might that be?

16. Ice demon from *Game of Thrones*

H: The person who came to mind was from a TV show, *Game of Thrones*. He looks like he is made from ice and he has these aqua-blue scary eyes. He directs his hordes—these zombies that come from the land of ice.[24]

Amy: Could you act like this ice-man with blue eyes?

H: His skin is translucent, and he is an ice demon. [closes eyes]. I am scared to look at anyone, because it is intense.

Amy: It is powerful. And while you are doing that, maybe you can sense what his spaces and time are like, in his world.

H: There is little space: it ends just above my skin, but there is infinite time.

Amy: Infinite time and very little space.

H: And time is sooo slow.

Amy: Thank you—you can relax now, if you want.

H: [wiggles whole body]

Amy: Now we will put that aside. Go into phase 4. Take a moment to relax, if you can. Relax your mind and body. Be careful of yourself and your movements and people around you. Just breathe a little, and just let yourself be moved by the space around you. Relax and let your phase 4 movement experience happen.

H: [moves very slowly, gracefully, hands and arms liquid in motion, head slightly tilted, torso turns 90 degrees and back, arms graceful]

Amy: As you move or are being moved, perhaps in that silence you can hear some sounds, vibrations, and even music in the air.

H: There is a tinkling of little bells. Like those flowers that look like bells, that wave like that in the air . . . I don't know how to make the sound of bells with my mouth. [Begins to make sound, a thin, trembling tone. Giggles. Moves between Amy and Arny with her little bell fingers]

Amy: Maybe we can all do that for a second [Group does it]

H: [laughs!]

Amy: Now, as you make those sounds, see if you can feel into the space and time of that X ice-no-space-infinite time thing. Somehow, this sound and movement will feel itself way into it and find out something about it.

17. Icelandic singer, Bjork

H: Well . . . something about vibration bouncing off hardness. . . . It creates these beautiful ringing bells. . . . It feels as if X is happening inside of the ice. . . . I am getting images of ice crystals . . . transmitting whatever is moving through it. Like using crystals for radio waves and signals. A kind of crystalline intelligence. . . . Oh, X's world begins to look and feel and sound like Crystalline—a Bjork song.

Arny: Explore and switch into that crystalline intelligence.

H: It is very sparkly, very clear, a lot of light, a lot of surface. [Someone in the room sings the music *Crystalline* by Bjork).

Amy: With that music and those sounds, note what the music is trying to say.

H: Ohhh! X's coldness and stillness is *not* the same thing as inertia! The *stillness is required to let things move through, as a kind channeling. . . . You have to have stillness to channel!*

Arny: Oh, wonderful! Stillness is required to let things move through.

Amy: Can you imagine how you might bring that into your life? How it might inform you about your sense of depression, the problem you were talking about?

H: Two things are coming. One is the hardness of structure. I get into the sense of needing to close myself, when life gets very big. It feels like I am getting depressed, but now I see—this is a *restructuring myself to be like those bells. It is a hardness or stillness, so something can move through.* If those boundaries were softer, then nothing will be able to move through . . . that stillness is not dead.

Arny: So—what you called a depression is actually a deep inner state of a quiet: a crystalline intelligence to let things move through you.

H: Yes, it's there to emanate those things!

Arny: You got it. . . . So, what looks like a depression may be a hidden gift to emanate! Can you imagine using that emanation power, now?

H: The meaning and the depth behind what looks like a problem may be a hidden gift and power and brilliance waiting to come out. Now, my question is: how can you get to these insights when you are in it? . . . I actually got out of years of depression by allowing myself to drop into it even more. I gave myself 2 months of "You can do whatever you want, just doing nothing." After about 3 weeks of that allowance, energy returned.

Arny: Yes, going into that stillness may be the beginning of creativity. What looks like a problem may be a gift in hiding. Thank you, H!

The big point she showed is that what looks like a problem— with *the light of music*—appears to be a hidden gift. What looks like a depression may be the beginning of channeling awesome music—and more.

How many have found that what might be a problem might also be a gift, in the background?

One student realized that he could bring the magic and fun from his inner work into his teaching, making the classes more fun, too! In a way, you never have to leave home; you are never gone. Don't ever leave home, even if you go abroad. Live IN-SIDE-OUT.

Remember #4, the processmind, and the sounds and visions giving you light. This incredible experience is often associated with the gods. Your light and sounds are always available. You can depend upon that. In your 2nd Training, just practice momentarily sinking and singing into the X, to illuminate it. Light, in the form of spontaneous wiggling, movements and sounds, is always there to help.

You can go to other people to have them help awaken that in you, but you know how to do it yourself. Encourage other people to know that they are the wise ones, too. Help them to realize their wisdom.

The universe is your best teacher. Remember your own wisdom. As you are moving, notice repetitive movements, listen for vibrations or tones or sounds in the air. Let them emerge and hear their messages.

CHAPTER 7
The Sounds of Silence

• • •

WE HAVE SEEN IN THE prior chapters how processwork's phase 4 light, sounds, and music help us to communicate with our own worst inner problems and troublesome individuals and organizations. Connecting to our deepest and often marginalized essence level spirit creates *wonders*.

I want to thank my teachers for stimulating me towards processwork discoveries. As the pictures to the right show, I am indebted not only to our clients around the world but also to our witchdoctors and psychological teachers.

I value both being realistic and following the magic messages of inner and outer worlds. Quantum physics and Einstein's ideas about light helped to illuminate the 2nd Training, to communicate with difficult states of mind and difficult people.

For this development and inspiration, I am thankful to Amy Mindell, and to all our friends and colleagues, and to all my teachers. Seen in the pictures are the healers from the *Giriama* tribe in East Kenya. I have also gained many insights from other Aboriginal peoples: the Haidas in Canada, elders from Australia and Brazil, and the Rinzai Buddhist group in Japan.

I am thankful to the Swiss Jungians, Dr. Franz Riklin,

Dr. M.L. von Franz, Barbara Hannah, C.G. Jung, and to the ancient Taoist teacher, Lao Tse. I am also grateful to the biblical figures like Joseph and his coat of many colors, and to my science teachers—symbolized by Einstein's curved space-time. I also thank the many individual and group clients from around the world, seminar and worldwork participants, business groups, government and U.N. leaders, for affirmation of processwork methods.

Now, I want to integrate the insights from the last chapters on light with a large worldwork event that happened in Greece, 2017. Worldwork is about people meeting each other from around the world to work out personal, social, and political issues and learning how to get along together in large groups.

Why was the world created with so much conflict? I recall the Biblical God pretty much saying to Eve, "If you don't do the right thing, I am

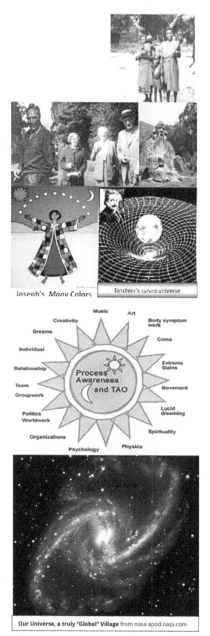

18. Collage of appreciations

going to put you on Earth as punishment." Is punishment what we are doing here? Whatever the answer is, here we are! We experienced a lot of tensions (and solutions) in a recent worldwork seminar in Greece.[25]

There were about 550 people (and it would have been 650 if there had been enough room!). In any case, many people from more than 50 different countries got together and worked on many issues. It was most remarkable for the fact that there was much conflict and also, much coming-together. For example, imagine many Latin Americans trying to awaken North Americans to the fact that "America means this whole continent. Not just the United States!" Imagine Africans trying to awaken Europeans to marginalization. It was all amazing. It was not just yelling at one another—there were also understandings and resolutions, as well.

MAINSTREAMING

We all need more multi-cultural thinking, wisdom, courage, and light. Mainstream people tend to center on mainstream cultures. They imagine their cultures are central, and of course, they are not. They are only part of the story.

I noticed we all have a tendency to mainstream ourselves. For example, if you stand in front of 10 or 1000 people, instead of being your normal self, there is always a tendency to adapt to others. I wondered why you sometimes don't believe enough in your deepest self? Instead, we look at the outside world and wonder, "What do those people out there expect of me?" We tend to *mainstream ourselves.* You put on a clean shirt, comb your hair and so forth. Regardless of your color or culture, or wherever you are coming from, we all wonder, *"How should I be, relative to the world?"*

I call that tendency to adapt "mainstreaming." You get up in the morning and think, "How do I look?" Some mainstreaming is needed and normal, but if it goes too far, you start to marginalize your deepest self—and inner difficulties arise, because of that.

Outside is important, and use your 1st Training skills for that. But your own dreaming light gives you the necessary 2nd Training directions that ease the tension. You need to be aware of all the peoples and issues around you, but without internal focus and dreaming, you get mainstreamed, and feel afraid or inferior.

However, there is a 2nd Training enlightened leader in everyone: a leader inside all of us, trying to move you and me. If we miss this inner leader or eldership, we become uncomfortable.

I am thankful to the Giriami group for modeling the needed 2nd Training inner work. This leading shaman-woman worked with her husband and child together. She would start to sing, and go into an altered state, "Ooohhhh!" Then her husband would get scared: "Hey! Don't go too far!"

She would continue to dive deeper into herself, then emerge, and say amazing things. She said to me, "You don't need healing," although I thought I did.

As I reported in earlier chapters, she went into the same altered state she had in working with us, and walked over to the people from her group who had been standing around, assembled there, during our healing. Then she *used the same state of mind to heal them.*

She showed that in the 2nd Training, the deepest part of you is needed not only to work with one person, but with the whole community. The 2nd Training helps everyone. That state transcends gender, nationality, age, sexual orientation, race, religion, and history.

Everybody is equally brilliant when it comes to this deepest self. It has to do with your seeing, hearing, and feeling *body vibrations of the essence level.* Remember, they are the sensations that are there before there are dreams.

HEARING ESSENCE VIBRATIONS

19. Simon & Garfunkel (Thanks Wikipedia)

If you really meditate and get to know yourself very deeply, you will rediscover that before there is a dream, there was a buzz. If we speak about complex things like quantum physics, we need music to make ourselves sane again. Listen to this song from Simon and Garfunkel:

"Hello, darkness, my old friend,
I've come to talk with you again,
Because a vision softly creeping
Left its seeds while I was sleeping
And the vision that was planted in my brain
Still remains
Within the sound of silence . . . "

The sound of silence! The basic idea is that *silence has a sound—a message.* From the sounds of silence, light, vibrations, light, and sounds emerge. Be in touch with the *sounds of silence,* the pre-dream condition. These subtle vibes tend to self-reflect and later appear as dreams.

The dream is like an image, an idea, or a feeling that you can almost formulate when the essence level, the sound of silence, reflects on itself and emerges. Later, we will feel this pre-dream as a movement that happens without vision or reason and then begins to amplify itself until you begin to see a dream image. Then you can say that you dreamed this or that.

But as I have said before, to say that you did not dream at all last night simply means that you are not in touch with this pre-dream state. This pre-dream state is a special attitude towards dreams. This state reminds me of the song, *The Sound of Silence.* How can silence have a sound? Silence has a sound, as we know from the previous chapter, when we do not marginalize, but sense this very subtle #4 pre-dream experience.

Recall that math of quantum physics is self-reflecting. Remember Richard Feynman, in the first chapter of this book, who said, "We don't understand the mathematics of quantum physics. It just works, so don't think about it!" Which makes some of us think even more!

As I said earlier in this book, the self-reflecting found in the math of physics implies that something in our universe reflects or wonders. This characteristic is not just in your personal psychology; as far as we know, it is characteristic of everything in the whole universe. Everything has this self-reflecting quality.

In our universe, everything may have the power to reflect and experience everything else. This reflection is part of our essence level, the subtle sound of silence, phase 4.

IRELAND

I have talked about this essence state in previous books, in connection with Ireland. Amy and I were working in Dublin just before the end of the severe conflicts between the Protestants and the Catholics, there. The leaders of the two main opposing forces were screaming—louder than anything I have ever heard. They were really yelling, each wanting to injure the other.

Amy and I were in the middle, trying to facilitate, but there was so much emotion and so much shouting, I couldn't think. Everyone was screaming, pressing towards the center of the room, where two men were yelling at one another.

The emotion was so severe that I lost my normal state of consciousness, and everything I had ever learned. I am not sure what happened to me, and even before I knew about the 2nd Training and #4, the situation knocked me out. I felt nervous, I was shaking, and then, I let go entirely. Then, when I looked up, I saw for the first time, the neck of one of the men fighting in the center. He was a very light-colored man with a very, very red neck! I simply said to him and the group, "Ohhh! Your neck is so red!"

But I had to scream that, in the middle of everybody else screaming, "YOU HAVE A RED NECK!"

To my shock, he said, "Yes! My doctor said I wasn't to come here today, because I have lethally high blood pressure and if I go into this conflict, I could die."

Then suddenly, the man opposing him on the other side, screamed, "*You? You* could die? My doctor told me not to come because of my heart! *My* doctor told me *I* could die!"

The whole screaming room of people quieted down as these two men stood there in shock, looking at one another. After a few minutes, they came closer to one another and, realizing they could both die, they embraced in the middle of the room, with hundreds of people around them.

It was an indescribable conflict resolution moment. Their screaming—everyone's screaming—knocked me out into the essence level. Essence level intelligence saw that very irritated red neck.

They came together by themselves. I didn't do much at all! Awareness happened as a 2nd Training experience, without us yet even knowing about the 2nd Training. We need to remember that being knocked out into #4 is a marginalized state, potentially full of wisdom. The essence is an intelligence with a lot of light, a shaking dance, wiggle and sound.

The Shaman-healer, Don Juan, speaks of the Nagual. The Northern Siberian people speak of Shamanism. There are all sorts of ways of dropping down and picking up what you find.

DARKNESS

I want to go slowly over the song, *The Sound of Silence*, again with you.

Hello, darkness, my old friend. How can darkness be your friend? Darkness is an old friend. Don't ever forget it!

I've come to talk with you again. What is that about? What is it saying? Darkness, our old friend, is coming to talk with us again. Why is the song saying that?

Darkness is not as bad as we think. It is your old friend. When you are in the dark about something, when you don't know what to do—*not knowing can be a friend.* When you are at a loss about what to do next, remember this state is an old friend, something that will eventually illuminate you.

Because a vision softly creeping. . . . How does a vision softly creep? In your dreaming, in your sleep, it is trying to creep into you, to awaken you.

Left its seeds while I was sleeping. How does a vision leave its seeds while you are sleeping? Little tiny flirts are seeds of dreams.

And the vision that was planted in my brain . . . Now, this is too much! Who the hell planted a vision in your brain?
It still remains—within the sound of silence. The capacity to dream is always there.

Yes, I want to thank Simon and Garfunkel for reminding us of the sound and light of darkness! Their song is trying to reawaken us to the essence level and the light of our processmind. We are talking about music but also psychology, shamanism, quantum theory, and this quantum wave function, all at the same time.

THE METHOD

So, now comes the *Stop, Drop, and Note* method.

Let go and drop into the deepest self, the quiet self—and let the mediumistic part of you show the way. What I mean is: *stop.*

Then, *drop* your normal way of thinking for the moment. Watch how you move and wiggle and take *note* of what happens.

If processwork asked Simon and Garfunkel, "How did you and the universe get here?" What would the singers say?

In my mind, they would say, *"Hear the sound of silence, to reflect and create a Big Bang . . . that wakes up you and the whole universe."*

I think we experience the creation of the universe in #4. Every morning, when you have a dream, it is a wake-up call, so to speak.

STOP, DROP—DANCE AND WIGGLE

We might metaphorically call this pre-material pre-dream state "the sound of silence." If you are in touch with this state, you will never completely mainstream yourself.

If you are ever afraid of hundreds of people, or of speaking out, or of writing something, or if you are afraid of talking to people for whatever reason, do this exercise first. It is a good medicine for that kind of problem.

The idea of this exercise is to Stop, Drop, Notice sounds, and Dance. Notice what light, what sounds, what images, and jitterbugs come out of you. You will get little movement-like jitters, and then enter a movement meditation.

EXERCISE: STOP, DROP, AND JITTER DANCE TO FIND YOUR 2ND TRAINING LEADERSHIP (alone or in dyads)

1. Choose an inner or outer problem to work with.

2. Standing, or sitting at the edge of your chair, STOP + DROP—(i.e., let go, as if sleeping).

3. *Note the phase 4 empty, relaxed, somatic, non-image experience.* Catch, follow + unfold subtle body feelings, movements, images, and sounds. Unfold those movements carefully, but expressively, as sounds, movements, images, and feelings.

4. Now, let those relaxed body feelings, sounds, movements, and image self-reflect. That is, dream into and associate meaning to the dream sounds and feelings. Make notes about your answers.

5. Remember the problem and imagine how those inner experiences answer that problem. Make a note about this.

6. Helper: Play the problem out that you heard the person describe and encourage that person to use their deep #4 processmind experience to resolve it. Then, helper act out the person's everyday "me" with the

problem. Meanwhile, you who are doing this exercise: be the processmind, giving *you* solutions from essence, like sounds and experiences. Make notes, because what you are doing may be far from everyday consciousness.

Here's an example from working with C.

Arny: Now, is there an unsolved inner or outer problem that has been bothering you?

C: It is an outer and an inner problem—it's my father. He is 81-years-old and he is not in good health and I don't imagine he will be on earth for long. He has been going from Canada to Costa Rica, back and forth, because he says his "real" sons and daughters are in Costa Rica. . . . He has five children, three from his first marriage and two from his second marriage. Most of them are in Canada. But he does not talk to my sister, my brother and now, one of his other daughters. He is very bitter.

Arny: Why doesn't he talk to them? He doesn't like them?

C: I think my Dad has a lot of bitterness and anger, and often he is childish. He feels, "Fuck them all! They can all go to hell!" I found out he was hospitalized while I was in Greece and I called. He said he does not want to be here on earth anymore! I want to do something to help him die better; not so lonely . . . and he listens to me. I would like to help him to create what he wants and connect with his family. Perhaps he can get the love that he really wants.

Arny: How to get your father to relate better, make him happier. Since you are standing, try to relax and let go, as if you are a little bit sleepy. Carefully relax. No longer imagine anything. Let yourself just follow your body—let it move the way it wants to. Now, catch and follow tiny feelings in your body, regardless of what those feelings might be doing.

C: [goes inside and starts to sway back and forth]

Arny: Follow those sounds, feelings, and movements.

C: [Swinging back and forth. Hands, hips, move more. Catches herself as she goes forward, then back]

Arny: Follow your movements until some of them may begin to repeat. Aha.

C: [sways, follows hands trembling, sways more . . . Keeping balance, stops swaying and focuses on the arm motion, and amplifies that motion.]

Arny: Yeah! That is it. Amplify that arm until you know what it is you are doing! And you can make sounds, too.

C: [growls, while making the movements. Then whines, shaking. Then starts laughing] *I feel like a big brown bear! And I am shaking my Dad!* . . . Get it together! . . . I want to say, "If you want me to stop, get your shit together! . . . I cannot sustain this! I can only do it for a little while!" . . . I feel like this power is my bear.

Arny: Beautiful. The bear shakes the father up, "Get your shit together!"

C: As a bear, I would SHAKE HIM. Hey, Dad! You have got to get it together. BE A DAD! And stop being a child! . . . Call your children, listen to how they have been hurt, say you are sorry, make amends and get the love you want. Heal yourself and heal the relationships!

Arny: WOW! . . . I am now going to *play* C. You are going to be the brown bear. [As C] I have a problem with my father, I don't know what to do with him. He doesn't get along with anybody. He makes a mess with his children!

C: Grrrrrr! [To C played by Arny] STOP TALKING! Just shake him up and LOVE him! . . . Be the him that you imagine you want.

Arny: [as C] I like you as a bear. *I need to pick up your energy when I deal with him.*

C: It's funny. My body feels like a bear from the waist up. I think when I did that as a bear, the powerhouse in me is one with love.

Arny: Your 2nd Training, phase 4, bear-powerhouse love says, "Get your shit together!"

C: That is love. It is true.

Arny: Everybody be a Brown Bear for one minute!

Group: GRRRRRRRRRR!

C: [laughs] That is good!

Arny: Your 2nd Training reveals that power emerging from you.

C: Yeah! We all need to be it.

Helping the person to get in touch with their own 2nd Training wisdom in that #4 experience, then encouraging them to live and integrate that dreaming, is the point. Having worldly problems is difficult. But perhaps those problems are a hidden gift stimulating us to listen to our own "sound of silence," to quote Simon and Garfunkel. Perhaps problems are trying to get us into #4 to see the light and use our 2nd Training!

PART III

2nd Training in Worldwork

. . .

In chapters 8 and 9, I stress the practice and experience of Deep Democracy's 2nd Training as a Facilitator's Art, preparing for personal, group, and world issues.

In chapter 10, I introduce new self-check worldwork exams, which I created with Amy for the 2nd Training. These new 2nd Training exams encompass Inner Work, Relationship, and Worldwork.

8. **The Process Revolution Spirit for Small and Large Groups**

9. **Big TOE Revolutions for Large Groups and Governments**

10. **2nd Training Self-Exams for Worldwork**

CHAPTER 8

The Process Revolution Spirit for Small and Large Groups

· · ·

I SPOKE WITH AN OLD friend of ours, a processwork teacher and student of mine, Dr. Grady Gray, a few days before his death.[26] We did not talk about life or death, we just talked about a recent dream he'd had while he was in the hospital. (Thank you, Grady, for letting me talk about this). He had dreamed that the sun came very close to the earth and then bumped into it.

While we were discussing his dream, he asked me, "What is that sun doing?"

I said to him, "That shows you are in the process of an illumination—meeting the sun, detached; the power of illumination."

He was so happy about that, he forgot everything else. I said, "That is the point of whatever is happening." A couple of days later, his earthly form was gone.

I have worked with many, many people just before they died. Again and again, even in their very last breaths, those who could still speak most frequently talked about some form of illumination or next steps.

In all the cultures I have worked with, illumination or light often happens at the end. Now, Grady was always working on integrating illumination into everyday life—but the reason I am bringing his story up now, in the beginning of worldwork training, is because some part of you has a tendency to be illuminated— and to illuminate our earth—even though you may not feel it all the time.

In the previous chapters of this book, we saw that there is some form of essence-like light, illumination, or wisdom inside all of us. This deepest part of us is not just a wonderful meditation experience but a needed state of mind: an illumination. This light is the core of the 2nd Training needed to help our world.

To create a better world, I suggest continuing to focus on your own deepest inner work, even while doing small group and large group processes. Our goal is to use the 2nd Training to illuminate and help the problems at hand. In chapter 10, this training will be the goal of self-assessment exams. But don't get nervous: this will not be an exam in the ordinary sense. It is really a *self*-assessment—*you* will be checking how *you* are doing.

That exam will ask how you deal with people and groups interacting with you. That exam will also focus on your abuse issues, because those often get re-awakened in public, making it difficult for you to facilitate.

SOCIAL AND SPIRITUAL RANK

The world needs you and me to model facilitation. For example, consider rank issues. I am a light-skinned person. I am a man, a heterosexual, and from the USA. I need to mention those things to begin modelling rank consciousness and to create awareness for others with less social rank. Don't forget to speak about your social rank in a way that feels well to you as a presenter. My point is to speak about yourself in terms of social DIVERSITY ISSUES, to remind yourself and others about low and high social rank awareness.

Also notice spiritual rank. Having been hurt by mainstream society for one reason or another (as most people have), there is pain—and also a desire to change society. This desire gives you a spiritual rank or power that other people may not have. My own past social pain gives me a spiritual push and a bit of power. Facilitators, like all of us, should use our spiritual rank with as much awareness as possible.

If you have some social rank, don't hesitate to publicly criticize yourself and follow the conflict process between you and other parts of you that may dislike your social rank. For example, an inner or outer figure might say, "You good-for-nothing white male, Arny!"

Each in their own style . . . do it your way. I just want to recommend social awareness.

Other things give me a lot of spiritual, social activist rank. I have spoken about having been hurt as a child when people assumed that I belonged to a "bad" religion and therefore wanted to kill me. That was 1945. They said, *"You have to die!"* So they tied me to a tree and threw knives at me, aiming to stab me to death.

It took me many years to recover from that. Interestingly, I went through a whole Jungian analysis, and the subject never once came up in a dream. My personal history only started to come back to me when I was strong enough to deal with it. Then, I felt the need to work with groups, and not just individuals.

So, each of us may have some potential spiritual power associated with past social agonies. Past agonies are terrible, and at the same time they may give you awareness and a push to change our world, a push that others may not have.

As you know, 1st Training concepts can be discussed. However, the 2nd Training concepts are partly an art needed for sustainable social change.

RECALL THE PHASES

Everything changes. Remember phase 1: enjoy life. In phase 2, notice conflict: "I am tense, and upset. I am troubled! We are in conflict!" Try to solve it, work on it; but if you are open to this phase and expect it, you won't get stuck in it.

I loved my teachers in psychology but they suspected or hoped, as in many spiritual traditions, that if you worked on your problems, you would become whole. You integrated problems and became free! You were enlightened!

Yes, work on all problems; but in the 2nd Training for fluidity, the more fluid you are with your own and others' agonies and ecstasies, the better you will be in working with organizations, realizing that everyone and all groups go through phases.

Hating conflict is natural. However, with a processwork 2nd Training attitude you can flow with things. Then you will be better at fighting in #2, and taking the other side you're attacking or being attacked by, in #3. See life in #3 occasionally through the other's eyes. Then, your opponents will go with you more quickly, and not just hate you for awakening them.

Remember phase 4: detached, fluid, flow. Sometimes you wake up tired. Or you wake up depressed, and think, "Oh, no! Why go on?" From the larger viewpoint, fatigue and depression may press you to let go. Then you can feel deeply in yourself and let it move you. *You* need not *do* things, simply let your deepest phase 4 and the 2nd Training nature do them.

Don't just be down on yourself if you feel down, but go further down, and let go. If you are exhausted, that can also be a good thing. Yes, of course take a nap. Being tired can be a quick way to go deeper into your detached, phase 4 and 2nd Training.

The 2nd Training attitude is open-minded and understands that all relationships and/or organizations go through *all* phases. If you can occasionally have this generous process attitude, you are doing well with your 2nd Training. If you can be fluid, and consider that enlightenment itself is a phase and not the goal, you will be more open and fluid with yourself and others.

I understand that most spiritual traditions try to make a state out of enlightenment. From the processwork viewpoint however, #4 is a phase, not a program. Remember #4: to be more detached—even from that!

Revolution for me, means revolving. *The 2nd Training is a revolution in the largest sense.* It is about revolving, phase-awareness, and flowing.

I have introduced the 4 basic phases in my book, *CONFLICT: Phases, Forums and Solutions.* Now, let me differentiate those phases, increasing them from 4 to *8 phases.*

Phase 1. *Relax. Take it easy.*

Phase 1 ½. *Something (call it X) is beginning to bother you.* You realize, "Oh, something's bothering me, but I don't want to think about it!" Take a deep breath, meditate; but even after that, you might think, "Oh, that damn thing is back."

Phase 2 *is a state of conflict with X.* "Let's run away or attack X!" Then, after you have been in conflict, or after an organization has been in phase 2 conflict for a long time, phase 2 ½ occurs.

Phase 2 ½. *War Fatigue.* You are getting exhausted with conflict. You cannot take it anymore: you are sick of it, you're exhausted. You are fighting, but losing energy. Conflict feels like it costs too much.

Phase 3. Now you are closer to your dreams and find you can *switch roles with that X in your dream and see things from the other's viewpoint.* "Now, I can see things from the other side and can understand my opponents."

Phase 3 ½. In this phase, you can *listen to, or even befriend,* the other side. You are a bit more relaxed, because *you know how you are like the other.* #3 ½ allows some detachment, leading to phase 4.

Phase 4. *The sense of relaxed detachment:* a temporary phase, like all the other phases. Often, this phase happens only at night, in dreaming, or it tries to arise through taking drugs. In any case, this sense of relaxation and oneness is linked to many spiritual traditions. In process terms, however, it is not a goal but a phase: of being at one with all things. This phase leads to phase 4 1/2.

Phase 4 1/2. The feeling, "Oh, this is *such a great state of being! Maybe I could make this phase into my main reality so I can avoid everything!*" This phase happens just before returning to Phase 1. In 4 + 1/2, there is the sense, "Wow, this detachment is great! If I can just meditate deeply enough, problems will go away." But of course, #4 is not a state, but a phase—that leads on to phase 1. . . . And around we go again, on the process wheel.

You can also skip phases. Their rotation as I describe it is not a rigid rule; just an overview.

In the 2nd Training, centering as much as possible in phase 4 allows you to appreciate the process, and flow best with all phases. Phase 4 is a phase—and at the same time, the center of other phases, because from the viewpoint of #4, all the other phases are seen as natural and OK. #4's view is that everything is fluid: not permanent. From phase 4, flow becomes easier as you open up to the other phases.

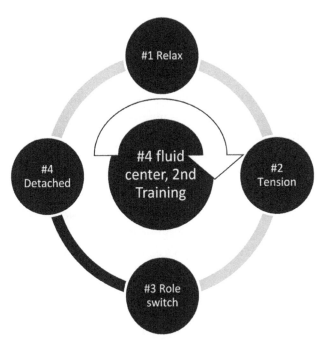

**20. The 2nd Training is a key to our health,
as well as the health of our communities.**

ARE THERE GOALS IN CONFLICT WORK?

That depends upon the time, the group, the world, and the issue you are working on. Try to hear and follow the group's goals and phases first, and remember that all individuals, communities and relationships eventually need process awareness of all phases.

A background goal for our human race is to create better, less tense, *sustainable relationships*. I am interested in the process of *Uniting* Nations, not just a fixed United Nations. *Uniting* stresses the process and not any one phase or state or goal. Our world would work best if we create the awareness needed for *uniting* nations, not just for a United Nations.

REMEMBER YOUR ABUSE ISSUES

As a facilitator, recall the deathwalk. If there is anything—about your color, race, religion, appearance, age, gender, sexual orientation, nationality, intellect, psychiatric or health issue—that does not fit into mainstream standards where you live, suffering frequently occurs.

Carlos Castaneda's teacher-healer figure, Don Juan, called the agony caused by the mainstream a "deathwalk." If, in a given community, there is anything about you that's not quite like everybody else, some form of suffering occurs, and you are in the conflict situation. I have been calling that deathwalk the lifewalk.

The idea is that if you must face, or walk in front of, others who don't like you, you are on a lifewalk. That is why many people get nervous as facilitators. Don Juan implied there is a way to survive it that can be helpful to others.

As you know from chapter 7, I call social pressure "main-streaming." You need your 2nd Training to get through it. To survive the deathwalk, you need your lifewalk. That is, you need to fight and wake the others up: "Wake up! We are different! Welcome diversity!"

Then, phase 3 can occur—at least temporarily—when you can see the world through the eyes of the other and understand them. Perhaps you are even like them!

But don't make a rule out of that phase 3. Remember it as a possibility. Following your deepest phase 4 and your 2nd Training will help you to remain fluid and be present with all that happens.

If you have been attacked, or have an abuse issue of some sort, you are usually extra careful in public. Even today, I am still afraid to walk down the street at night, past shadowy places. It was not until I went into phase 2 as a teenager and could get back at some of the people who were against me that could I relax, and later, even love them. But today I love them even more, because without them, I would not have the diversity interest to work with, and to help our world.

CONFLICT AND BODY PROBLEMS

Let's do an inner work exercise focusing on groups, organizations, and countries. As usual, let's call that energy of the person or people who bother you—the energy you are trying to get rid of— the *X energy*.

We shall connect that X energy with one of your body symptoms that is similar to the energy bugging you from present or past abuse issues, or times when you have been hurt.

Working with people over time, we noticed that what bothers you outside in the world turns up inside your body. This work should help you with any fears about facilitating worldwork situations and can also help you to manage inner problems, so you can use your abilities. We are going to ask you to find the X body symptom energy in the outside world, in a person or group bothering you.

For example, there is a group I would work on, where the person there is very mean, sharp, and pointed. Now, I also have recently stomach problems and sometimes I feel a real sharp, stabbing pain in my stomach. I have an acid stomach. Sometimes I feel this intense burning. This stomach pain reminds me of that person.

Then, we shall work with phase 4 to resolve issues. The idea is that if you really let go and are moved creatively, you will probably gain insights you might not otherwise have had in your ordinary state of mind.

EXERCISE: PHASES OF INNER WORK

1. Think of a family, small group, or organization which has a person or energy that bothers you. What's the worst person or X energy there, for you? Make a motion with your arms or whole body to express the energy of that X. What does that energy express? How would you describe it? Make a note about it.

2. How is that X energy in one of your body experiences or body symptoms as well? Make a note.

3. In what phase are you with X (in your body and/or in the group)? #1: ignore X, in #2: fight X, in #3: role switch, or #4: detached and flowing?

4. What personal abuse or hurtful situation does that X *energy* remind you of? Make a note. Did you, or can you now, imagine fighting X (phase 2)?

5. Stand, if possible, and let your body relax and be moved. (Be careful of your own body, your back, and neck). Wait for spontaneous repetitive motions. Let these spontaneous motions create a 2nd Training dance and tip, to help with your body and to help deal with the outer world X. Make notes about your spontaneous motions and their possible meaning. Imagine using this tip (your art) to help deal with that person, group, or organization. Make a note.

Demonstration of this work with Arny.

Amy: Choose a family, organization, person, group, or tribe where there is a person or group with an energy in it that bothers you.

Arny: I can't say the details, but it's a group that asks for help. They are doing good things in the world and I want to support that, but the leadership there is troublesome for me. I want to help them, but they are hard to work with.

Amy: What are they like? What is the worst energy or quality of that person that bothers you? What's the X energy?

Arny: The X is pushy, "You have got to do it now! You must help us! Come on! Take care of our business! This is important!" I have said, "Other things are important that I am working on, too." But they say, "NO! Our problem is the point!"

Amy: Make a movement to show that X energy.

Arny: I love their goals, so I want to support them, but . . . their energy! "You have to do it now! Do it! I want you to do it! Do it!" [makes punching motion] I agree with their overall direction, but some of that punch is a little difficult to get along with. Behind their request is a punch, "Help us!" [punches air towards Amy]

Amy: Make a note about that energy, the disturbing X energy.

Arny: [Draws a squiggle that becomes an arrow: a big, pointed arrow head] It is complicated. You want to help, but the people who are asking you for help are pushing you away at the same time.

Amy: Are you aware how that kind of X energy is in one of your body experiences, or a body symptom you have? Do you have that kind of feeling?

Arny: Well, now, I don't have high blood pressure, but I have a sort of—ppfff! Feeling of pressure.

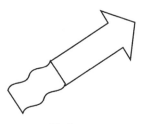

21. Arrow

Amy: What phase are you in, with that X energy? Inside or outside phase 1? You would love to ignore it?

Arny: Yes, mainly! Drop it. Do not think about it.

Amy: Phase 2 would be fighting.

Arny: Yes, I have tried that. It didn't work yet.

Amy: Phase 3—taking the other side?

Arny: Never! I mean, yes, I tried that too, but it was only for two seconds. It wasn't enough. It did not go well.

Amy: Phase 4? Detached? Flowing?

Arny: No, not yet.

Amy: Is there a personal abuse situation that that X energy reminds you of?

Arny: That X reminds me of my childhood. Yes, my abuse issue is probably why it makes it more difficult to work with that group.

Amy: Were you able to fight that energy, in that abuse issue? Or can you imagine doing that, now?

Arny: At that time? It took me 15 years, and I did. But fighting is not working here, with this group.

Amy: So, now, we are going to go to phase 4. Let your body relax for a few minutes. Drop all the problems for a minute. Relax, and let your body be moved spontaneously. Relax and be careful of any physical limitations. Don't hurt yourself, but let your body be moved spontaneously. As you are doing that, wait for any repetitive spontaneous motions that come up. You might have different movements, but some of them might tend to repeat.

Arny: [makes a downward, then sudden, sharp uplifting motion with his arm] That is it!

Amy: Notice your repetitive movements, and let your empty mind give you a 2nd Training dance tip for how to deal with that X energy in your body, and the X outside in the group you are working on.

Arny: It is coming . . . Shut up! I love you! Shut up! Now, let's work together.

Amy: Shut up. Let's work together. Can you imagine how you might use this?

Arny: I must say, "Let's be quiet, that's enough for now. I do like you. Now, after a break, let's work together on the big project. . . ." Wow . . . that might work with this particular situation.

Amy: It looks like you're picking up the X energy itself, the "bang," so they may feel met.

Arny: It is a paradox. I must say, "It's enough for now!" And say, "I am with you, anyhow! We are in the same boat!"

Amy: How would this help you with your body symptom? Not just the outer situation?

Arny: The sense of inner pressure is due, in part, to my not letting the pressure out. My sense of pressure is not due only to them. It is due to my not letting my pressure out—barking and woofing, like a dog would do!

T: Arny, you mentioned an abuse issue. You went inside and experienced that. Can you go back and show how that is helpful?

Arny: The abuse issue was having been beaten and stabbed; pushed against a tree, and tied up to that tree, with people stabbing me. That was an abuse issue, yes! So, being pushed around reminds me of that issue.

Amy: You said, earlier, that in a way, you were able to fight back and later embrace them. It sounds very similar to this process.

Arny: Wow! I did not realize that. Yes, that was right for me. First, I had to really woof back, and later, I could really love them.

Now everyone should try the following exercise.

EXERCISE: PHASES OF INNER WORK IN SMALL GROUPS OF UP TO 8 PEOPLE

1. Together *(10 minutes)*

   Choose a reader who will also participate. Each person *briefly* mention a group/organization problem that interests you. Can be family, group, or even a tribe you are part of. (Reader, write these groups/problems down.)

   Reader, mention each group/problem, one after the other, and ask everyone to make a sound to show their interest in working on that topic. Choose the group/problem that has the most sound or emotion.

   Person whose group/problem was chosen, say a bit more about the most difficult X person or energy in that group problem for you.

2. Inner Work led by Reader (*10 minutes*)

   a. What's the biggest X person or energy *for you* in that group or organization situation? (It could be the same or different from the one mentioned earlier).

Act out that X with your hands, face, and whole body. Make a note.

b. How is that X in one of your body experiences and/or body symptoms? Make a note.

c. In which phase are you, with that outer X? (#1 try to ignore X, #2 fighting or resisting X, #3 role-switching, or #4 detached). Make a note.

d. Let your body relax and be moved spontaneously. *(Be careful of your own body and those around you.)* Notice when movements begin to repeat—and sense your phase 4 dance and art: that is, your spontaneous creative motion. Continue to move and wait until your movement process gives you a spontaneous 2nd Training dance tip about how to deal with the group. Make a note. Then, imagine how this same tip might help you with your X body symptom or experience as well. Make notes. Share with one person.

3. Small Group Worldwork *(25 minutes) (Reader, read all of this before beginning)*

a. Person whose issue was chosen, set up 2 central roles in the chosen group/problem.

b. Everyone, act out those roles. Remember phase 3, and try role-switching. When you are ready, bring in your body work and phase 4 art experience and tip, to help you facilitate.

c. In general, try to stay close to that phase 4 art tip and fluidity, to elder the whole situation and to flow with all phases as they arise. Stop after 25 minutes.

d. Remember to try and represent the different sides and move back and forth between the sides. Try to bring in your body work and phase 4 tip to help you elder and facilitate the whole situation.

e. The general idea is to stay as close as possible to that phase 4 and its fluid dance to somehow elder the situation, and flow with all the phases that come up.

4. All together, afterwards *(10 minutes)*.

If time, discuss the use of your 2nd Training tip and fluid revolving.

Role-switching is something we can do at any time. We never need to be stuck. There is always room for spontaneity to come through—and magic can happen. In a way, some problems might be needed, just to teach us to be spontaneous and flow with processes!

CHAPTER 9

Big TOE Revolutions for Large Groups and Governments

· · ·

Peace is crucial, but not the only goal.
The larger goal is using awareness to flow with the phases of
relationships for more sustainable friendships. That awareness
is the key to the 2nd Training.

I WANT TO REMIND YOU that you have the best teacher inside of you. Your 2nd Training experience is the best teacher and knows just what is needed. Therefore, before beginning a group process, we should always remind everybody to realize that they are all *participant facilitators.* Each person is a participant and has leadership potential within them.

All of us are participants in group processes, but we also have facilitator ability to help elder the outer situation. Don't only empower other leaders. Empower and encourage yourself and *everyone* in their 2nd Training.

Whenever possible, especially as an identified facilitator, always notice the issues and most difficult X energies. Fight, and when you are ready, try to see through the eyes of an X person.

Do that as much as possible. Model role-switching. For the sake of community in our world, encourage both stepping firmly into roles and becoming fluid.

As I said in the last chapter, the biggest world problem is that, even though *we need you and me to facilitate world conflicts,* most of us avoid this and just fight in them. This is understandable and needed, but that is only a phase 2 reaction against a part of the world. Remember all the phases, and all the people.

Remember the Big TOE, the Big Theory of Everything. As I have said before, in physics, TOE refers to joining relativity theory with the theory of tiny quantum particles. Quantum theory and relativity are not yet integrated in physics.

Please recall, we are missing a *Big* TOE in our world that could bring together spiritual traditions with physics, psychology, world issues, and worldwork! We need a *Big* TOE, a Theory Of Everything—to involve everybody in making a change.

Our lives already integrate spiritual experience, medicine, psychology, physics, yoga, and worldwork. But we must help our religions to connect with the sciences, psychologies, and world diversity issues.

The 2nd Training and Big TOE see *everyone as part of your family.* I don't want to go too far with that phase 4 view, but it is important to have that view, at least now and then. Try to communicate with people, have a sense of where and who they are, instead of just seeing them as the "other." After all, we all live in one huge field, one planet, in our universe.

When you do worldwork with small groups and large organizations, remember at the same time that you are working with your body and everyone's internal processes and possible issues. All outer processes and energies are inside of people, as well. So, if you feel disturbed with something inside, it is an outer problem or energy, as well.

For example, just about everyone thinks about aging, at least sometimes. You might wake up in the morning, and look at this or think about that—what is the heartbeat doing? What's the rear end doing? Aging is a global problem. I am aging. I am 79 and can't avoid the idea of aging. Aging helps me, and perhaps you, to realize that we need to learn how to let go, now. Why wait until later? Follow your dreaming body. In a way, you and I will always be here. Death is a consensus reality term which you need to believe in, but there is a dreaming aspect as well. I remember the Native American, Chief Seattle, saying:[27] *"There is no death, only a change of worlds."*

My feeling is—yes, your physical form is going to die; but although Jung died, he is still here. The reason we came back to the United States from Switzerland is because Amy and I were in bed together in Switzerland, and in a dream, C.G. Jung came to us. He tickled our toes and said, "It is time for you to go to the US and become a leader there."

Did C.G. Jung die? Yes, and . . . No. In a way, he is always here.

Until now, we have talked about rank awareness, gender, race, health, color, looks, age, sexual orientation—all these things are important. I have also spoken of learning to feel into the other side X for personal and for large group processes.

Speaking out is terribly important. That is phase 2. We need more people in phase 2 to take a stand about diversity issues of all sorts. But phase 3, role-switching, makes whatever happens in phase 2 more sustainable. Recall that *revolution implies revolving through all phases.*

ORGANIZATIONAL RANK CONSCIOUSNESS

In organizations, phase 1 says, "We are doing fine! We are doing well again! Yay!" Yet, don't be surprised if #2 might be in the background. One reason is that if an organization is doing well, other organizations may not like that. Or members of the original organization who are lower down will struggle to be on top. So, it is important to be rank-conscious as an individual and as an organization. Rank unconsciousness in yourself and your organization creates internal and external attacks.

THE PHASES OF REVOLUTION

Organizations always wonder, "What is happening to us? Why are people inside our group fighting?" Or, "Why is another group trying to kill us?" The answer is, "You are in phase 1—where you don't want to think about problems or rank consciousness, and fighting in phase 2." When your group starts to get exhausted from fighting in phase 2, that is the moment for phase 3 and for communing with the other side. As I have been saying, it is time to learn to open up and facilitate.

On the global scene, there were some quiet years, and now it looks like things are changing. Expect change. Conflict is to be expected. Not because the world is evil or sick, but because the world is revolving. So, expect change.

REVOLUTION

Remember, the core meaning of revolution is "revolving." Watch out. When you are in phase 1, you don't want any problems; but don't be surprised when they come up in #2. In #3, explore communing with people.

Imagine Saturn's rings. In #4, become the ring that embraces the situation, the phases, our planet. There is a deep something inside you that believes that even though you might have been hurt and can fight back in #2, eventually you might embrace everyone involved, in #3. This view is not permanent, as is sometimes suggested by religions. Rather, the ring around the planet is a #4 idea of process. Let #4 come and go, when possible.

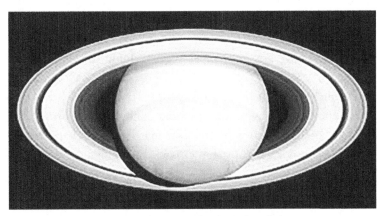

22. Saturn's Rings (Thanks Wikipedia)

Even if you have been very hurt by the world, your pain is a phase—and other phases are still possible in your dreams. At night, your mind relaxes and opens up, and you can dream about just about anything—be here for self and others, and also put your foot down and woof when needed.

#2 occurs inside of us, when we must fight mainstreaming that rejects minority characteristics. In time, eventually, things revolve. In #2, you have to be angry and fight. "Get that stupid idiot to know what they did!" When you hit them, and they are lying on the ground, so to speak, remember your #4 potential to be a ring around the planet and pick them up and make friends. No one is entirely evil or good.

ALTERED STATES IN GROUP PROCESS

In worldwork, in Greece, I recall one participant who got so angry about an issue, she went into an altered state in the midst of those 550 people. She began fighting and would not stop. She said, gesturing strongly with a pointing finger, and a crescendo in her voice, "*You* have got to change! We are doing the right things! Change!"

Because she went on and on, people tried to stop her, to no avail. They got so hypnotized by the content and words. So, I thought, beside the content of what she is saying, perhaps there is something important happening in her double signals and overall process.

I said, "Bravo! You have stopped us all from talking! You have such *power!*"

I said that because her wild body expression was saying, "I have an important viewpoint! Woof! Here I am! Recognize ME, a powerful person!"

So, I said, "Wow! I recognize that you are a powerful person!"

That quieted her down. Don't listen just to the words of people. Watch their body language and guess what it is saying and asking for. Her body was saying, "I AM POWERFUL!" We can all understand her. She seems to have been someone who has not been as powerful as others. So, in a way, she was begging for recognition.

In the middle of tense situations, we all get hypnotized. So, we need to come out of that consensus reality hypnotism and use our awareness to follow the body language. My point is that if you work with an organization or are part of a group that sometimes has trouble, work on their problem. Try to solve it, and remember the signals that the people or organization do not identify with. Those body signals are *secondary processes*.

LARGE GROUP PROCESS ON RACISM

Let's apply some of these ideas to a large group process. First, we will choose the topic. (In the example below, a vote was taken and the group selected *Race & Racism in the United States*.)

We will do inner work first. I will lead you through a quick inner work so that you can find your own phase 4 dance and tip for dealing with the issue. This might help all of us to be participant facilitators. At one point, we will try to read into the world of the X that is difficult for us, into their time and space.

2ND TRAINING INNER WORK ON WORLD ISSUE

1. What's the worst X (energy, person, figure) in the chosen world issue, for you? Act out that X. Make a note.

2. How might you experience that X (or its energy) as an inner problem? That is, how might you experience it as something against you? How is that X somehow a part of your life, inside or outside, in your own behavior? Make a note.

3. Imagine fighting X in phase 2. Maybe you have fought it. Imagine resisting, conflicting, talking to it, in your own way. Take your side strongly.

4. Whether your fight is successful or not, *try to commune,* and feel into the *inner or* outer X/person's signals in phase 3. Feel into their world a little bit—are you able to? Feel into their signals. What is their sense of time? What is space like for them? *Is it relaxed, spacious? Or restricted, in a rush? Endless time? Feel a little bit into*

their world. In what way are you yourself also X? Make a note.

5. Now, detach in phase 4—*stand if you can,* relax and feel the universe moving you. *Be careful* of yourself and others. *Watch your neck and your back as you move spontaneously.* Continue to move until you notice spontaneous repetitive movements happening and let them develop their own dance, sounds, or song. Then *let your spontaneous art/song/dance experience advise you about how to deal with the outer X.*

6. Make notes about the tip + briefly discuss with someone nearby.

GROUP EXAMPLE (ONLY CENTRAL ISSUES AND SPEAKERS ARE MENTIONED)

Al facilitated on the topic: "I am feeling my heart beating" on the theme *Race & Racism in the United States* (also referred to as "President Trump and White Nationalism").

Amy (to Al): Did you get an inner tip from your inner work?

Al: I saw my own face, which was weird . . . and . . . something else about my face was really kind, and that relaxed me. [Now to the group] Our issue is "Trump's impact on kids, white nationalism, white supremacy, police violence and specifically, killing of black men and women—and the institutionalized aspect of that." Who will speak first?

J: My grandmother was 77-years-old, a short black woman, light skinned because her grandfather was a white man, and she told me, "You are a pretty little black boy! I wish all my grandbabies were just as black as you are." In the time my

Grandma lived, she bowed her head to young white women who were my age. She said, "Yes, Ma'am" to them, so she knew what racism was. I said, "Grandma, you don't have to say that anymore," and she said, "Baby, in my day, we had to. In my day, if a black woman did not duck her head to a white girl, she could have died!"

Arny: The grandmother is a perhaps a ghost role: a background feeling, speaking about present situations today and racism in the past.

Al: Yes, and a cool spot occurred just now in the group when the grandmother appeared.

I: When you ask me, as a white person, to be an ally, to wake up to what is wrong, I think of all my own agonies . . .

J: (To I) However, even if you are completely poor, white people often consider themselves better because your skin is white.

I: Yes, and as white people, we have not turned to ourselves and looked at our history. We have not done our work on our own multigenerational trauma and white diversity, and so, we are unconscious of our effect on others.

[Many people speak until things cool down.]

Arny: We have been speaking for a while, and this momentary cool spot gives us a moment to stop, though the problem is far from being completed.

Afterwards: [Talking with Al about facilitating]

Arny: Wow. Everybody was shocked. Music and the grandmothers are in the air. Love was there and also lots of woof is there. Al, how are you doing?

Al: Personally, pretty good.

Arny: Talking right after something as a facilitator is almost impossible. I want to say thank you to everybody from the facilitation role.

D: Al did a great job. It was too much for any one facilitator.

Arny: The ghost role of the missing black grandmother could have been brought in more. She is the one who brings the pain of history and also love into the process. We all need to find such a grandma!

Al: The grandma in me also wants to say to everyone, "I love you guys and I feel so lucky that you are in the world and that our paths have crossed."

Arny: Al, how was all that for you, working on that as facilitator? Is it possible to talk for a minute?

Al: I noticed myself just kind of flowing with whatever came up—there were moments I got really pointed, which is a style I am working on more, in the moment. I am also getting more direct.

Arny: Yes, bringing in that direct energy as a facilitator is often helpful.

Al: If I amplified it more, it would look like . . . [he moves his arm forward, very directly and abruptly] I am going to practice that even more!

Arny: It looks good on you.

Al: (Playing a bit) Alright, everybody! I am going to practice with you all! Watch out!

Amy: I was relieved when you did that. It brought a lot of clarity and focus, because things get so wild. You brought out some of the really key moments. It was very relieving.

Arny: Yes! And that is my only suggestion: use your power and focus in bringing clarity about roles.

Al: Thanks to everybody for holding together, for facilitating together.

Arny: Thank you, Al. And everyone, remember to play out the ghost roles: people mentioned but not present. For example, that grandmother was an extremely important, wise and loving figure who suffered a lot and could potentially help with some of today's issues. She represents historical issues that have relaxed a bit, but are still in the back of everyone's mind. Also, the police appeared in the process, and getting deeper into the negative roles of the police towards people of color is very important in racial issues. The white supremacist side: a troublesome but important aspect of the overall work, is or was a ghost role, as well. We need to fight that, and when possible, hear it speak, as well. The police were mentioned, so they are a ghost role, but not quite present enough. No one was saying, "I am a police officer," so Amy and I brought them in. The biggest ghost role was probably the feelings and agonies of Black history in the USA. It takes courage and time to bring up history, because it has a real and dreamlike presence today, as well. In this group process phase 2, there was fight and woof! And some began to work with phase 3, picking up the various roles, black history, white police, to see change happen more quickly.

Let me encourage you to illuminate the dreaming or feeling background to world events. How? Occupy all roles.

2ND TRAINING IN SMALL GROUP WORK ON A WORLD ISSUE (in 6s for 1 hour)

A small group process demonstration occurred next. Again, on the topic of racism. Feedback on that was as follows:

D: My personal experience of racism holds me back in the world. If you are black, the world is a dangerous place. You might get killed. I just got out of jail last night. M had just arrived from Mexico and I went to pick her up from the airport.

M: I had just arrived in this beautiful city of Portland to see my friend, D, and to come to this event. We were five minutes from the airport, and a patrol car stopped us. The policeman said, "You skipped a light." And the young police officer asked, "Where is your license?" and said, "It smells like alcohol in here." So, they took D out of the car, and I had to sit there as they made him do all these weird tests. You must stand 30 seconds on one leg to prove you are not drunk. Eventually, I saw them handcuff D!

D: I asked them to handcuff me, to get it over with. They put me in the airport jail and then transported me downtown, where I was alcohol tested, and my score was 0.3, whereas drunkenness is 0.8. So, I was 5 points off. I told them, "I used to work in the jail system. You can't just take me to the jail. You have to keep me here." And they said, "No," so I went to jail and I was just sitting there. Then, next morning, I had to bring myself and M to this seminar. I had to get my car, take my kid to the doctor and so forth. I don't take offence. At the time, the policeman was doing his job, but at some point, he started using his white privilege. He knew I was not drunk. He knew I worked in the jail and he just did what he wanted. Once we were in jail, he said, "Oh, we have to let you out" and they did. It was all just a waste of my time. It was a supremacy thing. Not a white supremacy, a *blue* supremacy.

Arny: Yes, the police: a ghost role. Say I am the ghost role, the cop. What would you say to me if you could have a complete conversation?

D: Officer Boyer, what are you doing?

Arny: Trying to be a good cop.

D: OK, I understand you want to be a good cop, but do you know the difference between drunk and not drunk? The test shows I am not drunk.

Arny: If I smell even a little beer, I have stupid projections onto people, due to my personal history. I must hold you back.

D: You are fucking my life up. It is just humiliating. Putting the cuffs on me, taking me to jail, when you know that I have done nothing to deserve this. What is it with you?

Arny: Your feelings knock me out of the role-play and really speak to me. I was speaking so reasonably and intelligently.

D: He did become friendly. He didn't shoot me. He could have shot me!

Arny: This kind of discussion we are having, here, rarely happens. Just having that open small group discussion can help. D, I am very touched by your equanimity, your peacefulness in this midst of that painful situation. You were able to be in phase 3, to feel into and discuss with the policeman you don't like in phase 2. Thank you, D. We see from your power and your openness to the police that you are already a 2nd Training teacher.

CHAPTER 10

2nd Training Self-Exams for Worldwork

• • •

Now, let's explore the second training *Self-Exam*! This is not an exam in the conventional sense—it is a self-assessment, to check out how well you are doing with your own 1st and 2nd Training, and to update your own facilitator skills. I'll introduce it and demonstrate the self-assessment exam.

We need to remember again and again to flow with things: flow like nature, as the seasons' cycle and streams flow into other streams.

The 2nd Training is an art and an altered state flow experience created by letting go and being moved by the universe, the spirit, the field, God, or whatever you want to call it. The point is to wait for your own processmind intelligence to bring you tips that you might have overlooked in your "normal" state of mind. The 2nd Training helps you to flow with the phases by noticing and being open to them and having the eldership necessary to stand for change, and for everyone involved.

As I have said, flow is not a frozen state nor an enlightenment.

It is a phase 4 experience that appreciates the overall flow of nature. It would therefore be unnatural to be in phase 4 all the time. However, it is important that you remain open to and have access to, phase 4, when needed. Then, you can relax sometimes, even during tense times. #4 is a key to worldwork that reminds us not to wait until you go to sleep to dream. Dream in the daytime, too.

RECALL COOL SPOTS

When things cool down, remember what happened that allowed events to cool off. There are solutions hiding in those cool spots. Please remember that.

Remember both your 1st and 2nd Trainings. In 1st Trainings notice signals, double signals and hot spots. For example, when Obama was leaving office and Trump was entering, they were photographed shaking hands. See the picture of them below?

See Trump extending his hand, and Obama turning away. That is a picture of the U.S. today—many of us are like Obama, turning away from Trump. Obama's shaking hands and turning away are two separate signals, or what I call a double signal.

23. Trump and Obama (Thanks to nprnews.org)

WORLDWORK IN GOVERNMENT (AND IN PUBLIC)

A number of leaders I have worked with know about signals, double signals, and worldwork, but they often say they cannot use their knowledge because it is too new for the public.

I now realize that many worldwork concepts need to be taught in kindergarten, to help kids learn how to work on things. In order to learn worldwork in kindergarten, remember that whenever children have conflict, teachers should bring the conflict into the classroom. S/he might act out both roles and say to the kids, "What would you add or subtract?"

For example, the teacher might say, "On the playground today, there was a fight between this person and that person. Did you see that? I will act out both sides of the fight. "What do you think the opponents were thinking or feeling?"

Of course, this acting-out could also be done with puppets. It can be done gently, without disturbing parents or their cultures.

Each culture has its own communication style. In Japan, for example, touch on conflict briefly and gently. You can show the conflict work in 30 seconds.

Remember the 2nd Training and *don't work only for solutions, but also for improving relationships that make solutions more sustainable.* That is why I have been saying, "Don't work for a United Nations alone, but for *Uniting* Nations." They are both important, but the *uniting* is a process, not a fixed state.

Help others and yourself wake up. Make your point! We need all of us to stand for new ideas and more equality in societies. Make your point and help the public to awaken around issues of color, sexism, sexual orientation. . . . Wake up around race and gender, religion and ageism, and looks-ism, finances, health, and so forth.

Now let's begin the 2nd Training exam. This self-check exam is for people who would like to explore their own development in worldwork awareness.

Your intent to pass the 2nd Training exam changes the world, not just your success or failure at it. The following 2nd Training self-test can be done alone, or in twos or threes.

One person will be a reader. The u is the one taking the so-called exam. The third person can play the X: the problem person or group. To play the X, listen closely to what the u says about that X energy. Then, at the given points, the reader or third person will bring that X role into the dialogue. This dialogue makes the exam about flow, not just about facts.

The person taking the exam, u, will then show how u deals with that X.

Can u use the phases with that X?

Do the self-assessment . . . and enjoy it!

Exercise: 2nd Training (Self-Check) Worldwork Exam

Alone, in dyads, or in triads—25 minutes for each person. Switch the person being tested 3 times

- U is the one being tested.

- Let one person be the Reader/guide/timekeeper and play X (or let a third person play X) when needed, especially in questions, 1, 5, and 7.

1. *(maximum 5 minutes)* What worldwork situations (group, family, organization, community, etc.) do you love the most, and which ones do you like the least? Make a note. In that worst situation, describe the kind of person, energy or moment that is most difficult for

you. (This might be a real outer person/ figure/ group/ moment or a typical inner negative feeling towards yourself that comes up.) Make a note + call it X and act it out.

Now, 2nd (or 3rd) person, come in and act out that X. U who are taking the exam, work with X using phases 1 and 2. Also, try to commune and be fluid in phases 3 and 4.

After a few minutes, stop and rate yourself. How well did you do with X? (1 = poor, 2 = ok, 3 = good, 4 = great). Record your score.

2. In working on conflict and facilitating, do you notice double signals, roles, hot + cool spots, ghost roles? (1 = poor, 2 = ok, 3 = good, 4 = great). Record your score.

3. In general, can you fight in phase 2, and also be rank-conscious? Rate yourself (1 = poor, 2 = ok, 3 = good, 4 = great). Record your score.

   Can you role-switch in phase 3? Rate yourself (1, 2, 3, 4). Record your score.

   Can you sometimes be fluid in phase 4 and use it to flow with all of the levels and phases? Record your score (1, 2, 3, 4).

4. Are you able to commune (i.e., *read into* an X's space + time) in phase 3 when needed? (1 = poor, 2 = ok, 3 = good, 4 = great). Record your score.

5. *(maximum 5 minutes)* When you facilitate, what is a typical worst outer world or inner psychological X, for you? Describe and act out this X.

- Now, 3rd person, act out this X.

Now, work with X using phases 1 and 2 and in 3, try to commune with X and be fluid in phases 3+4.

How did you do? Rate yourself (1 = poor, 2 = ok, 3 = good, 4 = great). Record your score.

Person playing X, enter the scene and freely debate this rating, if needed! Person working, record your score.

6. *(2 minutes)* Can you lead and also be self-critical in public (as if an X was against you)? Imagine you are in public, and be self-critical now! How did you do? 1 = poor, 2 = ok, 3 = good, 4 = great? Record your score.

7. *(maximum 5 minutes)* What does your processmind phase 4 experience advise you now, for your future worldwork training? To find out, let go and get in touch with your phase 4 art, song, and/or dance and discover the message it is bringing. Make notes.

- *Reader + 3rd person, feel free to debate or add* comments about the person's future learning or training, if needed. The person working, please interact about that advice using your 2nd Training art. Record your score.

8. When ready, schedule a next (inner and/or outer) exam with yourself or others.

We ask you to rate yourself on how are you doing—either 1-2-3-4. 1 is not so good. 2 is a little better, 3 is even better. 4 is great.

We are not interested in the result. We *stress that your intent is more important than any number.* When you rate yourself, at certain points ask the other people working with you (the person playing the X and the person guiding you through the exam) if they agree with your rating. Feel free to debate them about their rating!

Make sure you make notes along the way. Take this exam for fun, once a month.

Exam demonstrated with K.

Amy (reading): What worldwork situations or conflict situations in groups, families, or organizations do you love the most, and which ones do you like the least?

K: At work in the hospital, I feel marginal, as a nurse. I don't know how to have relationships with the other nurses. They are my problem, my X!

Amy: Can you act out those X people, so Arny can play it?

K: Yes. The X says, "I have been doing this for a long time, and I do it really well—so you should work hard, and then take a break!"

Amy: The next step would be for Arny to play this X character, and for you, K, to use your phases. Use #1 or #2 conflicting, and then, phases 3 and 4.

Arny: (As the X, the quick, unrelated nurse) We are self-confident! We can do this work really well and quickly.

K: [looks at him closely]

Arny: I have lots of things in my pocket. No time to relate!

K: [Reaches into the X (Arny's) pocket!] Let's get to work!

Arny: Wow, you almost knocked me out! You were so natural and quick! I have never had anybody go in my pockets before.

Amy: Yes. K, as that self-confident X nurse, just went for what she wanted. OK, K, how would you rate yourself for going through your phases? 1 is poor, 2 is OK, 3 is good, and 4 is great.

K: 4. That is—great!

Arny: Did she feel into me?

K: Yes, in phase 3 I switched roles, and could feel into Arny, the nurse. I saw how you are focused, and how you can pick up what is going on and not get dreamed up into an affect. You just know what to do—you are so amazing! I want to be able to do that.

Arny: Oooooh! I am now on your side. You did good work! Let's do some more! The way you felt about me, and into me, dissolves my X behavior.

K: I think qualities you have are energies I admire.

Arny: What you, K, are doing, dissociated me from what I was doing. You brought me out in ways I cannot define. It was perfect!

Amy: Back to the exam. K, when you are facilitating, do you notice the 1st training structures?

K: Not so good. The exam score is 2. I have such a strong, feeling nature that I can get pulled in with groups. In a way, I sometimes lose my awareness.

Amy: Now the next question is: K, when you facilitate, what is the worst outer or inner X for you? It could be an inner critic telling you that you are no good. Is there an inner or outer person, or figure that is hard for you, when you are facilitating?

K: My inner critic tries to mainstream me, so it's often hard to facilitate because I freeze, trying to be like the mainstream way of doing things. I don't have enough access to my own feeling experience, and therefore it is hard to flow with groups.

Arny: What does that X, inner critic, do?

K: Mainstreaming. It gives me doubts about being a normal nurse. I also get self-conscious about my large body size. Right now, I am feeling pretty good—but in terms of raising my hand to facilitate, I think everybody is going to see me as big, and I get shy.

Arny: In terms of body size, what is the X saying?

K: YOU ARE TOO BIG!

Arny: I totally understand. [Now addressing the group] How many people have an X that looks at you negatively? Appearance? Skin color? Behavior? [Hands go up] Wow. Many of you!

Amy: Arny, if you can play that X and K, see if you can use phases 1 and 2 and commune with him in phases 3 and 4.

Arny: (As the X) OK, here I am. Hmmm, your size is big, and your clarity?

K: (to that X) Oh, I am so sorry. You suffer so much. It is not right.

Arny: I suffer as the X?

K: Yeah, you do.

Arny: Well, I am constantly trying to be perfect.

K: *You!* That is why you are so tense.

Arny: We must all be perfect!

K: No—you don't have to be perfect. You just have to have good intention.

Arny: (As X) Ohhhhh! You melt me! Thank you, K! You are beautiful! You could not have a better size or appearance!

Boy, she was enlightened! She really flowed with that conflict process and was able to commune with me in #3.

We are trying to teach that each of you is your very best teacher. From one perspective, life itself is a kind of dreaming, flowing, and relating exam, a tough but perhaps good one.

In all the different countries you come from, wherever you are living, help people wake up—bring out the diversity between u + X and help everyone read into the X. Encourage people to explore and get interested in tension and conflict.

Remember to revolve fights and create revolutions. Recall the song *Revolution* by the Beatles (written by John Lennon and credited to Lennon–McCartney).

The Beatles sang: "*You say you want a revolution. Well you know, we'd all love to change the world. You tell me that it's evolution. Well you know, we'd all love to change the world. But when you talk about destruction, Don't you know that you can count me out, Don't you know it's going to be alright? It's going to be alright!*"

PART IV

Nonlocal Psychology and Physics

. . .

CHAPTER 11

Waves, Particles, and 2nd Training Inner Work

· · ·

SOMEONE RECENTLY TOLD ME SHE had such severe pain that she wanted to die. She said, "I don't want to work on it. I just want to die. They won't give me enough morphine."

I said, "Don't work on it. How about just letting go, now? "

"What do you mean?"

24. Wave rider

"Let go, into another level of reality."

"Do you want me to die?"

"No, and also yes, psychologically," I said.

"How?"

"Carefully follow your imagination of letting go and dying . . ."

. . . "Oh!" she said. "This is better than morphine!" Then, she added, "My god! Now I know what I want to do with my life!" And we went on in that direction.

So, let me remind myself and you: *follow the process.* That is such a simple thing to say, but when dramatic things are happening, you think, "What can I do?" So, my advice is to be careful, be conservative, and then radical. With phase 4 and your 2nd Training, things will flow.

That brings me to the theme of this chapter: *Waves, Particles, and the 2nd Training.* I had a dream that the essence of Native American traditions is what we will talk about in this chapter. To me, that essence means caring for these marginalized peoples and their earth-based belief systems. Follow the earth, listen to the skies, and support the people.

Like our world as a whole, the United States is, and has been, unconscious about race issues. We need to realize that repressing people also represses their deepest spiritual teachings—which are very much needed today. So, we must care for the people, love and support them, and also recognize their brilliant traditions.

Most of us try to look like normal consensus reality people and forget our essence level where we are quantum-like waves, dancing around. CR belief systems are OK, but they marginalize the dreaming in ourselves and in all cultures.

Dying people, almost always, dream about the next steps. I have worked for over 55 years in practice with a lot of people, and have seen again and again that life often seems to go on for people near death.

The first very ill client Amy and I worked with together, many years ago, eventually went into a coma. As we worked with him, he came out of it the day before dying, and announced, "Oh, yeah! I am going to go study at the Processwork Institute in Zurich, next month."

What we usually call reality, including life and death, are consensus reality terms: not the whole story.

That reminds me of a conversation I had at the end of one of our seminars working on diversity issues. Some people came up to me and said that their minister had gone to a seminar we had given on racism years ago—working on agonizing diversity problems. That seminar came out very well. Their minister had said, "Arny believes in Jesus!"

So, they asked me themselves, "Do you believe in Jesus?"

I said, naturally, "I love Jesus!"

"*You* love Jesus?"

"Absolutely. His way is behind phase 3: turning the other cheek. That is the essence of role-switching."

"How does that fit Jesus?" they asked.

I said, "Instead of 'an eye for an eye'—reacting to everyone who is against you—we can go with Jesus and sometimes turn the other cheek, at least temporarily. So read into the other person's heart and mind, if you can." They understood.

My goal is to develop processwork in such a way that it fits, at least partially, into everyone's deepest belief system. When people dislike rank-unconscious white men, I understand and in a way, turn the other cheek and look through their eyes. Diversity consciousness, for me, means in part realizing that I am relatively white, heterosexual, male, and all of these mainstream things. So, I must be very conscious, and use my unearned social rank consciously.

In the processwork community, I want to use my rank to support other people and their viewpoints, and their ways of doing processwork, as well. Each of us has a little rank or a lot of rank, in one way or another. Let's use it consciously.

My point is that *your inner work is another form of worldwork:* what you do with yourself is a world issue. You suffer and/or enjoy world issues. But anything you do inside yourself has effects outside. Inner relationship work with inner figures melts into your outer relationship work—which is part of worldwork. In any case, worldwork does not work very well without inner work and relationship work.

If you want sustainable solutions, you must relate to the "monster" inside and outside. If that monster gets interested in you, you will have more sustainable results and world relationships.

The first step is to wake people up and the second step is understanding or even appreciating something about them, so they will eventually come with you. Create relationship, not just war. Be one-sided, and then open up.

Our present world paradigm today is, and has been, "I am the best and the other must suffer." Therefore, in processwork, work with the problems and switch roles, at least inside. Know that the group you are trying to awaken might be you, as well. Then, your results will be more sustainable. It rarely happens, and I don't push this viewpoint with everyone, but for those who want to facilitate a more sustainable world, all the steps and phases are important.

A first step is always to say, "Wake up!" A second step might say, "I have been where you are. I am waking up and I understand your life, so let's wake up together!"

This is not easy at first, and it's a matter of timing. Be both a realist and a dreamer in touch with the essence level. You, me, and the whole world often get stuck in phase 2 conflict. So, we need to die a little, get illuminated, and detach. I only succeed in doing that when I am a little relaxed myself.

Whether someone is raging about inequality, or lying on the street screaming for drugs or money, or sitting quietly in a meditation center, I want to, and hope you will also, try to relate to them.

If you start getting exhausted in psychological work or processwork, be careful with your health. But the idea that you are tired can also be positive; it can be used to go to phase 4. Be drained. Relax and take it easy. Even if you are worn out and you think you cannot do something, this could be a phase to let go in your work and fall into phase 4, especially in a difficult situation.

The big goal in the 2nd Training is to flow through all the phases. Work for better fluid relationships, as well as specific solutions.

QUANTUM PHYSICS AND RELATIONSHIPS

Remember quantum theory from the first chapters? It can help relationships. I will make the quantum theory for relationships simple now.

When you first wake up in the morning, you are normally relaxed, in phase 4—and you are closer to your wave-like breathing experiences. This is when you *feel* yourself at your deepest essence level.

Then you get up out of bed and you look in the mirror and think, "Oh, no! I see myself and don't look perfect!"

When you observe yourself, your dreamy wave-like nature becomes particle-like. Before you look at yourself in the mirror, you are still a bit dreamy and wave-like. Then, when you look in the mirror, your consensus reality self awakens. You wake up and like a physics observer looking at quantum waves, the waves become particles—that is, *things.*

One of the great physicists in the early 20th century (supported by Einstein and others), Louis De Broglie, discovered in 1924 more about the wave-like nature of matter. He explained that if you send a particle of light towards a wall and observe it traveling, it appears as a particle. And if you don't observe it, only God knows what reason it behaves like a wave. See the picture of this below.

Look in the Mirror, See a Person,

Feel Yourself as Your Wavy ESSENCE!

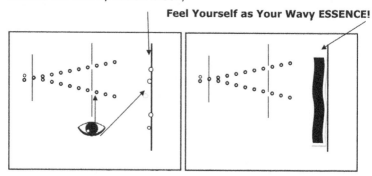

25. Observe, for particle . . . let it be, for waves

If you ask, "What do I look like? Do I have the right clothes on?"—you appear as a particle, a thing, a human being. But in a restful mood, you are more wave-like.

In principle, you are wave-like, and you appear as a particle or thing when looked at.

When you reflect, or wonder, "What is going on, in me?" you become a CR particle—a bunch of particles and parts.

When some people say, "I didn't dream," remember—you might not see a dream, but you can always *feel your wavy self*, as in pre-dreaming. *The wave is a pre-dream essence experience.*

A dream appears as we observe that wavy essence-like experience, and dream images emerge in dreamland. Sometimes it is hard to recall a dream in part, because the dreaming process is still in a wave-like form.

A particle is the thing-orientedness of the wave: a graspable consensus reality thought or idea, preceded by deep, wavy feelings. Looking at a wave, or self-reflection, allows particles to emerge in our physics, and in our psychology.

The 2nd Training in terms of quantum physics suggests: Don't repress your wave nature. The wavy part of us is easily forgotten or neglected, and that makes us afraid of illness, makes us depressed, and so forth. It makes us fear weakness.

Now, let's re-consider the Big Bang—and update our thinking about how our universe got started. Until now, nobody knows how or why our universe made a Big Bang in the beginning. All we know for sure is based on the light beams we receive, allowing us to measure back to about 13.8 billion years ago. Then, we find a Big Bang happened—when particles started popping up. There are speculations that there may have been things even before the Big Bang—some of my friends at MIT and Harvard have been thinking that way—but there is no empirical proof, yet.

In my book, *Quantum Mind*, and in the first chapters of this book, I suggested that the universe is curious and self-reflective. It has a tendency to awareness. This leads me to speculate that the universe began because of its self-reflective potential: a potential we notice in quantum theory and in our psychological tendency towards self-reflection and consciousness.

Quantum theory indicates *a reflecting tendency* in the universe. It is possible that the universe wonders about itself and created its own Big Bang. It awakened, as a thing, from its wavy, dreamlike world condition. Perhaps this is why, for centuries, many have said, "Maybe there are gods or goddesses in our universe."

Perhaps the universe's inherent reflection and illumination were or are projected onto the gods. Perhaps that is why I dreamt about Native Americans recently, to support this ancient belief that the universe we live in has a potential for awareness.

What does this Quantum Physics mean for Psychology? Many things! But at the very minimum, 1st Trainings need to be devoted to consensus reality and learning specific things. 2nd Trainings are then about letting them go, becoming wavelike, feeling the deepest flowing part of you, and flowing with that. 1st Trainings are social and cognitive: focused on signals, facts, roles, rank—as we have been talking about.

2nd Trainings involve dealing with reality and sensing the wave-like, relaxed phase 4 experience, and from there, taking the next steps. If you can do that occasionally, you will be more creative, spontaneous, and help yourself and others.

I spoke about this in chapter 7, in terms of Simon and Garfunkel's music: *"Hello darkness my old friend, I've come to talk with you again."* Musicians and everyone have had a sense of the wavy background, this darkness that precedes everyday consciousness. The Buddhists help us to understand this, by focusing on the wave-like nature appearing in your breath.

You can go to a meditation center to focus on that and/or just remember to breathe in and out. That is one of the fastest ways to get in touch with this essence level.

SAMADHI

Some Buddhists call this deep breathing experience "being one" with everything, or *Samadhi* calmness. It is a peak experience, a kind of unity with the divine. It is awareness of the essence level.

Following wavy essence level feelings is a Samadhi-like experience: following your flowing nature, the waves of your heart beat, your breath, waking, and sleeping. I don't think we tend to go to sleep just because we are tired. *What we call tiredness is a need to get in touch again with that wave-like part of ourselves.*

It can be very important to be asleep and then—WAKE UP!—as the sleep state *moves you* in waking life. We need to flow between being particles and waves.

THE BIG TOE

Such ideas begin to draw the psychologies, spiritual traditions, and physics closer together to create a TOE—a Big TOE (a big theory of everything).

To begin with, be a particle and a wave. In both psychology and physics, the wave-like part of you is a pre-dream essence experience. When the wave wonders about or reflects on itself, images and dreams get created and new realities are offered to you in reality!

THE OPPOSITES

If C.G. Jung were here, I would tell him that getting in touch with our deepest essence-level wave experience can bring what he called the "opposites" together. Being in touch with your #3 particle + #4 wave-like breathing nature relaxes tensions and brings opposite sides of your personality together as different aspects of one flow.

What looks like opposites aren't—from the deepest wave-oriented process view. This idea of opposites is particle thinking. That is OK, but it is not enough. From the deepest viewpoint, the essence or wave viewpoint, there are no things—just phase 4 flowing waves: essence experiences.

Being in touch with waves is both a personal and a social issue.

I think of myself as a male. If I look at myself as a particle, I have a penis I never talk about, but it is there, with some other attending things that go along with it. I have a brain, and I look more or less like whatever a man is supposed to look like today. And if you are a woman, you have breasts, and your body curves a bit more than most men, and so forth. That is a particle view.

But my point is that *from the wave viewpoint, you are neither male nor female, gay, straight, Black, Yellow, White, Asian, African, European, and so forth.* You are a fluidly changing mix of all possible types of people.

Agonizing social issues are due in part to the rigid CR particle viewpoint. It is crucial to wake up and work with those views and change them, to open up to our incredible diversity.

So recall the wave view: we are waves flowing between the diverse forms. You may look like a man—that's fine; but unless you are in touch with the wave-like part of yourself, you will be that one man, alone—and you will marginalize other people and other colors and other ways of relating, sexually. The wave-like part of you will make you realize that, at the deepest essence level, you and all of us are flowing rivers.

The particle view is important, and the new marginalized essence-wave view is crucial to being process-oriented. The wave view, our deepest experience, can temporarily help us to detach and gain some release from social issues.

Divide things up into parts and particles, but don't forget this wave view. We are male, female, dead, alive, and fluid.

The masters of wave-like consciousness are children. Watch little kids. Kids are amazing waves. As we get older, we marginalize our wave-like nature . . . except when we dance and sing. It could not be simpler than that. I had to study quantum theory to understand kids.

It is normal to play and swing and have a good time, instead of having to be a particle all the time. All that fun is about wave consciousness.

A WAVE EXPERIMENT

- Sit or stand, and get comfortable.
- Notice your breath, your breathing.

- Don't only breathe, but let your breath organize the movements of your tummy, your stomach, your hips, your neck. . . . You may not be used to doing that. It just takes a minute.

- Let your breath organize the way your stomach and back move.

- Let breath organize the way your head and neck move a little bit, breathing in and out, so that it is breathing-dancing in your own way. (Careful not to hurt yourself.)

- Neck, hips, stomach, shoulders, too, can swing. Get to know the wave-like part of you. This may bring you a little bit into an altered state. That is OK—we will be working with this state later.

Get to know that wave-like part of yourself. Be wavy as much as possible (except when you are driving! Then, be one-sided ☺).

Thanks to all who teach meditation. Thanks, Fukushima Roshi, the head of the Zen Rinzai sect, who said, "empty mind is creative mind."

We can now say, *Empty mind is wavy, creative quantum mind.*

NONLOCALITY

Because you are quantum-like—you are also a bit nonlocal. Nonlocal means that things you think of and do in this state might possibly be connected to or even helpful to someone at a distance. You may be connected to telephone calls before you get them.

This is a quantum aspect of psychology. Perhaps people in this wavy state are nonlocal. Nonlocality is something to discover, not to believe in. Get into that state, and see how it works at a distance.

Now, let us *use this state to focus on the client-therapist practice situation.* When you work with somebody as a helper—whatever the work you do—notice that 95% of the things that bother people are due to mainstreaming. That means people feel pressured to do things in a mainstream way: act right, have the right color, hairstyle, lips, the right body, and so forth.

Mainstreaming is a consensus reality human story, and can be very painful. There is a lot of cultural pressure behind the problems bothering people. That is why I said that worldwork is inner work, as well as large group worldwork.

As a therapist, notice mainstreaming agonies within racism, homophobia, sexism, religion-ism, health-ism, age-ism—and other isms. This is because people who feel they are not acceptable feel ugly, sick, or crazy. Look at those things and take them seriously, work with the edges and the details you have learned from processwork and other methods. If they work, great. Otherwise, remember *phase 4: that is, relaxing and meditating, and let the wavy processmind show the way.*

We are going to do this in an exercise. We will work with things as best you can, but also stay in touch with this wavy part of yourself. Get into this wave-like #4 state and let *things* pop up, with new creative ideas to help yourself and your clients.

In the exercise, we will be working with *chronic problems and difficulties.* The therapist is important, but *the client is the best therapist.* They don't need you as a therapist! The clients have the wisdom in themselves. Never forget that *the client is the best therapist.* Look at them that way. (Also see this in you, when working with yourself.)

This work will support all helpers to be mediums and see if your nonlocal wave-like experiences help the client. Here is the exercise.

INNER WORK DYAD: 2ND TRAINING CREATIVITY (AS A MEDIUM) WITH A CHRONIC PROBLEM

Helper read:

1. Client, show your worst chronic or present problem and its troublesome X energy. What is your normal u like? Make notes—and sketch their energies.

2. Meditate . . . and feel into phase #4. Go into wavy darkness. Breathe. Sense the quiet, the stillness, the slight wavy motion-feeling and sound. Let slight, spontaneous repetitive motions happen. Let those motions sketch themselves.

3. Feel/see/guess what this sketch advises for that X problem and note the advice on paper.

4. Now, helper: Yourself, do the above steps 2 and 3, with client's X. Then explore, using your 2nd Training creative wave-like breathing experience and art with X, for solutions.

5. Afterwards: Ask client if your art-advice was nonlocal and helped the X problem.

It is important in the beginning, as helper, to listen carefully to what the client says their X problem is, because I want you to go into wavy darkness, feel, and sense what advice turns up. I want you to use that 2nd Training art to see what *it* advises for your *client's* problem. I want to show you that we might all be a bit mediumistic. Check with the client whether it works.

Demonstration with H.

Arny: Show your worst chronic problem X. What is the worst problem that you are always working on? I am sure everyone has at least 10 to choose from.

H: To deal with the stress . . . waking up in the morning with 25 things on my list and this constant [big eyes, a lot of movement with hands!] problem: how to survive that or enjoy it. How to switch off and relax, when there is so much pressure and so many things to do! I love the people part of it. It really matters to me. It makes me cry. And I am scared to let people down. My symptom, in the moment, is a tight shoulder. It is squeezing and pressuring me to work harder! [She shows two fists, one on top of the other]

Arny: I got it! X says, work harder! That is X! So, X is uptight and nervous? Can you draw that, there?

H: [Draws a tight spring, coiled, shape] Work harder!

Arny: What is your normal little u like?

H: I don't know. Maybe that stress *is* my normal state?

Arny: OK, X is your normal state. Let's now explore the wavy darkness part of you, your breathing. Those who feel able can help her by breathing, too. Let your breathing move you a little bit. Breathe deeply and let breathing move your stomach and your hips a little bit.

H: [eyes closed, moves her neck, her back, her knees. Sways, head flops forward, then up]

Arny: Walk about, like you are—breathing, wiggling and moving, and see what sort of spontaneous little motions might come up.

H: [Stumbling backwards, she begins to spin and smile]

Arny: When you are ready, let this loose movement sketch something spontaneously on the board. Let your hand go wibbly wobbly.

H: [draws several circles]

Arny: While wiggling, look at that for a moment. What does that sketch advise the more coiled up, tense, anxious one?

H: The circles say, "Enlarge. Make it bigger!"

Arny: [Acting like the everyday H] How do I do that? I am so uptight! What do you mean, bigger?

H: Make the anxious state bigger! OH! My nature is normally small, coiled—*I am trying to be small!* [She explodes outwards!] That is a relief!

Arny: How might this wave-like advice look, in a job?

H: Like this [H shows hard work: very tense. Then slows down, looks around]. It is playful. It is important to go deep inside, so you can explode out. Yes! Then, there is a lot of space for everybody. There is also something about helping everyone to feel part of this big thing. . . . Yes, feeling everybody . . . I like working hard. It is fun. But I like this expanding to include everyone, as well.

Arny: Two minutes ago, the problems looked like hell. Now, it is fun to work so hard when you explode and include everybody.

H: [nods] Oh, yes! Thank you.

Arny: Now, I will work on H's process by following my own nonlocal experiences. So . . . the X said, "Work harder, H!" But now I am going to follow *my own second training art dance.* I breathe a little bit, move around a little bit . . . and notice what it does to me. [Makes wobble-arm-motions]. It is similar to H's, but a bit different. My process says, "Yes,

H! Hooray! And hooray, everybody!" It is close to yours, but something also wants to say, "Hooray to YOU!" What does that do, if anything, for you, H?

H: [Jumps high] Yay! I am getting bigger. Hooray!

Arny: Instead of being all cramped up and nervous, twist and expand! Hooray, everybody. Hooray, H. Applaud yourself! Feel prouder and bigger!

(To the group) Did you get the idea? Your dreaming may add something that could be useful for the other person. Your interpretation and feeling about the experiences may not be exactly the style of the client, but it might be helpful. Consider your work as an offering. My processmind experience was to applaud her getting bigger! Her problem is nonlocal—it is mine as well! We all need more support and love and pride.

Next, the whole group did the exercise. Afterwards:

Arny: Could any of you put words to your experience?

R: I think I got the most out of it when my partner did my X energy and became Wavy Gravy. [Wavy Gravy is an American entertainer and activist for peace, best known for his hippie appearance, personality, and countercultural beliefs.] I loved watching my partner's Wavy Gravy. I said, "Ohhh, I feel good already!" because my X was very tense—not like Wavy Gravy! I was super tense, and she was now doing this Wavy Gravy and I said, "That feels really good. How is it

26. Wavy Gravy
(Thanks Wikipedia)

for you?" and she said, "It feels really great!" and then said, "Take up more space! Be big, take in more stuff."

Arny: She thought of herself not only as a particle, but as a larger wave-like experience that turned into Wavy Gravy for you.

R: It sounds simple, but it had a profound effect on me, watching her get into her experience. On a personal level, I realized I grew up in a large family. So, when she said, "Take up more space, be bigger, expand!" it struck me really hard, personally, because my mother was terminally ill, and they were always saying, "Don't act up. Don't run around the house. Don't speak up!" So, what my partner did and said, now, was very powerful for me, emotionally.

Arny: [to R's helper, N] Are you normally so psychic?

N: No. I am so shy.

Arny: If you were not shy, what would you say if *you* yourself were to take up more space?

N: Oh! There you go! I got the message!

Arny: Perfect! *The client's problem is nonlocal.* What looks like a problem isn't only a problem. You are not just one person, especially from the wave viewpoint. You are nonlocal, part of a larger situation.

Anyone else have something they might share?

D: T was working on the X of tiredness. And my 2nd Training experience was an "Ommmmmm." So my advice to his X was, "You know, if you keep working at this, you are going to burn out." The image I saw looked to me like a Buddhist monk's beggar's bowl and the message for me had something to do with humility. And my helper, T, said, "Oh my goodness! I have been wanting to work on humility for a long time."

Arny: Oh, wow. That nonlocality is remarkable! Maybe we are not just one local person sitting inside our skin, but part of a nonlocal field capable of understanding and empathizing with everyone. We are not just particle-like, that is, in one spot or one body. Perhaps we are nonlocal and wavy, allowing us to understand and help others, as well.

CHAPTER 12

2nd Training Relationship Art Beneath Double Signals

· · ·

HALF THE TIME, EVERYONE LOVES relationships and the other half of the time we don't, because of complications. Perhaps quantum physics can help our relationship skills?

Remember, a quantic entity or photon is both a *particle* and a *wave* until you choose how to measure it. How we look at things partially determines how they appear. Of course, the same holds true in relationships. How things look depends in part on how we look at another person.

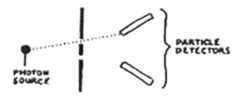

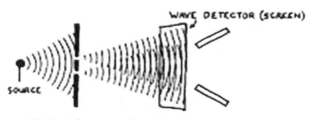

27. Particles appear if particle detectors are present.
Otherwise, waves appear from the photon source.

In any case, recall that waves become particles when observed, and that perhaps we are both, rather than one or the other. Note the upper picture, where there is a photon source sending particles through one of the slits. What began as particles end up detected as either particles (in the upper picture) or waves (in the lower picture).

If the wave-like form of particles is observed after they pass through the slits, they look like particles (as in the upper picture). Otherwise (as in the figure below) they appear as waves! Whether we observe particles or waves depends on the observer.

If you look at your dreams, parts and particles appear. If you deeply feel your nature, wavy feelings are experienced at the essence level.

What you see depends upon how you look; that is, the state of the observer. This observer effect is one of the great physics discoveries and mysteries of the last century. If you remain in consensus reality and look, waves become particles. If you feel and don't look for images at essence level experience, things are a bit wave-like. What appears depends on how it is observed. In other words, the wave and particle effect is not just physics, it is psychology, too.

HOW you look determines, in part, what you see. Before you look at yourself first thing in the morning, you might feel and observe wavy feelings; but when you look at yourself trying to get ready for consensus reality, you become a person-particle!

At night, if you awaken and try to remember an experience—you probably see a dream with parts. If you just feel, you notice wavy feelings and you might say you did not dream at all.

In earlier chapters, I suggested an apparently self-reflective ability in our universe. Perhaps, when the universe wonders about itself particles appear, and the Big Bang shows visible particles. In other words, self-reflection creates things—perhaps our visible Big Bang universe!

Now, think about this. If you identify only with the "I"—or yourself as a particle—you are a person. Here you are. You have to wear the right shirt, make sure it is clean—so, you behave like a particle.

The wave part of you is very different. The wave part has essence-like qualities. It gives you a wavy, Samadhi-like quiet mind, a sense of union with a divine-like feeling. Now, I want to bring this essence-like quality into relationships.

WAVES IN RELATIONSHIPS

Not everyone remembers dreams. But as I said, you always dream, in the sense of experiencing wavy, essence-like feelings. Remember the religions and spiritual traditions that focus on breathing. If you can, remember to breathe and flow occasionally; if you can bring some of your relaxed, sleep-like, wavy breathing quality into awareness, you will experience your wave nature at the essence level as well as its messages to enrich your life and your relationships.

How do we integrate that wave nature? Remember, getting tired can be the beginning of deeper wave-like breathing. Perhaps fatigue is due to getting tired of being too particle-like. In other words, what we call fatigue might be a tendency to re-experience our wave-like breathing. In this sense, fatigue can be a wonderful gift.

You can be a particle for a time: do this, do that, and when you can't, you can get closer to your wave nature. When you get tired, the waves are calling. It is very simple and new to think this way, but it's almost obvious. There are a lot more details, but I am simplifying things.

Waves and particles are phases we go through. You will recall that phase 4, the essence level at the center of everything, is wave-like. Then in phase 1, the particle appears: "Here I am! Wake up! Let's get going. I am ME!" In phase 1, you might still feel a bit of Phase 4.

Then, you might say in phase 2, "I have an X, and want to fight my inner or outer problems." But if you feel your wave-like nature, you can fight and flow between sides in #2, and even go to the other side if needed, in #3 and #4.

The 2nd Training is about flowing with phases—remembering this deep wave-like part of yourself, even when you are troubled inside or outside.

To study particles, just watch the news. Worldwide, most cultures teach us they are particles and in #2, fighting other—bad—particles. *Be stronger! Get famous! Get rid of the bad people! Otherwise, you are not strong enough!* Such ambitiousness is a phase 2 aspect of the particle's life. It is an important phase in human life.

Most modern cultures ask us to be a specific person relaxing in #1 or fighting in #2. Yet, to integrate the universe on earth, to help our little planet, we need to be particle—relaxing in #1 and fighting tension in #2—*and* wave-like in #3 and #4.

1st Trainings focus mostly on #1 and #2. 2nd Trainings recall that you and others are wavy, nonlocal spirits. If you don't remember the 2nd Training, you may get stuck in #2, afraid of an X person or X problem, or of getting an X disease.

But perhaps these fears are subtle ways to awaken you to get to phase 4's *waviness.* That waviness is good for many things and is surely good for your health. In phase 4, your body relaxes, at least temporarily. You can breathe deeply, and you are more relaxed, wavier, and temporarily more fluid.

It is important to fight sometimes, to take your side and say, "woof!" But then, if you hurt the other person, don't forget phase 3—flow over to their side.

The essence or phase 4 wave-like level in relationships is neither you nor me, but "us." That is a big point for me. When I realized this, I dreamed I was re-opening the doors of an ashram, and the churches and synagogues and meditation halls, all for at least one day a week.[28] #4 is the essence aspect of most religions; the powers in back of the images. #4 is a core of 2nd Training flow.

We will soon explore #4 and practice a new art, found beneath relationship signals. When we get to this phase, we are neither you nor me, but nonlocal waves, or the music and dance that connects us.

First, let me try *to get to my essence in relationship* to you.

HERE IS THE EXPERIMENT

The essence level experience is [Arny moves slowly, takes several deep breaths] . . . *so interesting. I am experiencing water. I am something like the sea. And that sea water wants to reach out and support everyone. In the moment, I want to give you a lift. I am the water that lifts and supports your boats, your people.*

For me to remember that essence level experience of wanting to support you is different than if I just explain, or teach, or get information across. The feeling of supporting you is more essence-oriented and closer to the experience of what I will call the nonlocal "*us.*"

28. Water that "lifts"

Finding this "us" is the key to our next exercise. Finding that "us" with someone else and doing it in public takes a moment of self-allowance. It is a meditation connected to your breathing. I sometimes do this on the street.

Amy reminded me that I did this essence experience in relationships outside of Starbucks on 23rd and Burnside in Portland, Oregon. We were about to drink our coffee and noticed that everybody had moved away from one free table. So, we thought, "Great! That's our table!"

But then, when we were about to sit down we noticed, right next to our table, was a strange person: a man in an altered or extreme state, who was almost naked. He barely had pants on. He was making very aggressive and intense motions with his arms. He was having a massive conversation with some invisible spirit. He was strong and kind of scary and everybody had moved away. There was one table next to him, and I said, "Let's go there!"

Amy thought, "Great! OK!"

We sat down, and noticed this guy had a stinking smell. That made it hard to stay there; which, together with the scary things he was doing, had probably pushed people away. He was talking out loud, going on and on, and he looked very aggressive.

Then, Amy tells the story: "Arny dropped into his own essence level. It was all a little scary, because I did not know what Arny would do.

"But suddenly, Arny said to that guy, 'God loves everyone! God loves everyone!' Arny said it a number of times, and suddenly the guy turned around. (He had been facing the wall, gesticulating), and said to Arny, 'I got to talk to you!' And he sat right in front of Arny, and said, 'You think God loves everybody? I got to tell you about God.'

"The man then asked Arny, 'Are you a minister?'

"And Arny said, 'OK. Yes!'" And then, this following conversation occurred.

"The weird man asked, 'Does God love everybody?' Then, he told us that the devil had come to earth, too. Then, he told us that his mother was a great woman. He said that when he was a child, he had fallen from a great height and hurt himself, but he was still able to learn to tie his shoes. Then he showed us how he tied his shoes. This man was 55 or 60 years old!

"We had a 5-minute conversation about God, then he turned away and he started to take his clothes from the shopping cart and put them on, in the most exact way. He had been very disheveled. Now, he started to put on his clothes very carefully. He was getting ready to go and became very quiet. He did not say anything anymore.

"We got up and Arny put a dollar in the man's shopping cart. That guy looked at Arny and said, 'Thank you!' And he grabbed Arny's hand. I started to cry—it was so touching. His look had changed, and the man was so touched. He had become very quiet and inward. It was all so very beautiful."

Thanks, Amy. My point is that dropping into the wave-essence level helped me relate to that person. There are other ways to work with extreme state situations by picking up signals, but this essence level work brought me the feeling that God loves everybody.

As Amy said, he smelled so much that normally it would be hard to love him. But we became great friends.

The essence level is linked to the experience of your breathing and brings you to possible nonlocal connections. When we were close to that man, I did not know what that essence would do. I was not *doing* anything. But he did change and was in another happier state of consciousness.

#4 is a wavy part of me, and it is part of all of us! Everybody has this potential.

At the essence level beneath relationship signals, there is a possibility to illuminate the key to relationships. Meditate on phase 4 breathing and explore your phase 4 nonlocal experience results.

This essence work reminds me of Rumi, the Persian Sufi mystic. He said about relationships:

> *"You and I have spoken all these words*
> *but for the way we have to go, words are no preparation.*
> *I have one small drop of knowing in my soul—let it dissolve*
> *in your ocean."* [29]

Rumi senses the other person has their own field and he wants to melt in with that. Then he speaks of himself:

> *"A mountain keeps an echo deep inside*
> *That is how I hold your voice."*

Can you imagine somebody saying that to you? Chances are, you would like them. This essence talk sounds romantic. Rumi was showing aspects of the #4 essence-oriented 2nd Training in relating.

Meet people, talk with them, work with them, use all the details you have learned and *remember phase 4 deep breathing and stillness. Let your neck and body relax. Let "it" move you. When you get to this deep essence aspect of relationship with somebody, it may also help everyone around you.*

The point is #4 essence level nonlocality has nonlocal powers. The 2nd Training in relationship involves meeting the other, talking about things in consensus reality, noticing your body signals, and dropping into phase 4 if you can. Revolve around the phases and bring phase 4 into your momentary relationship.

If you are having an argument, "I can't stand you" is OK, but at the same time, recall, "I am with you forever!" Let all those phases happen, and believe me, you will have less relationship trouble.

EXERCISE: YOU, ME, AND US

There is a simple meditation method that can help us in relationships. I will now describe it.

Sit comfortably, notice and focus on your breathing. Don't forget to let your neck be a little flexible and move as you breathe, just a little bit. Let your stomach or hips or back move a little tiny bit. A little movement is enough. Let your breathing be your dance instructor and organize your moments.

Now, as you move, perhaps some images from the resulting breathing experience will appear.

The images that come up are important. Catch one or two.

If you found an image, make a note about it. What state of mind does this image remind you of?

Feedback after exercise.

Arny: How many of you could find an image in there? Most of you! Who would share one of those images?

A: It was water. Not a river, more like a small creek, near the origin of which, water was flowing out. Yes, it was a spring, the water starting to flow.

Arny: The water is a symbol of the essence level; in your case: the beginning of a little river, a creek. Beautiful. That is you!

SK: I saw a little tiny plant, growing out of a rock wall.

Arny: Wow. What seems like the rock wall has life in it!

E: Mine was a building up of water and then—woof! Water splashing and crashing over, then building up again, and then words came: "It is all rounding."

Arny: All rounding. Your inner wisdom is in that "splashing"—round and flowing.

In this #4 state, we are all a bit like mystics, flowing together—at least temporarily. I imagine that flowing in relationships like the wave people in the essence level wave picture.

ESSENCE IN RELATIONSHIP EXERCISE

Next, we shall talk briefly about your signals or double signals. Then we will *investigate the stillness, the quietness, the breathing inside of you. We will focus on that phase 4 essence experience in order to process a relationship.*

We are going to meet with somebody, discuss problems, and center on essence level experiences.

29. Essence level wave experience figures (Thanks Shutterstock)

EXERCISE: THE ESSENCE: FISH IN THE SEA RELATIONSHIP

This can be done with 2 people: 1 will read. Both discuss possible shyness, discomfort, or a possible problem. Note rank differences and then go deeper to the wave level (fish in the water level).

Each alone: Note a double signal you make while discussing problems. (A gesture that suggests something partly felt, but not expressed fully). Speak about that double signal.

Now, both relax, drop into the essence. Imagine being a fish in the sea. Feel and swim in water and in the waves. Feel the fish's relationship to the sea. Breathe, move, feel, and swim it. After a minute, explore how your fish-wave essence nature experience may be the nature or art behind your double signal. Note and sketch that essence feeling on paper.

When both are ready, one after the other briefly share the essence experience beneath your double signal—and the relationship message/s trying to arise from that essence or quantum realm. Were the messages of both people the same? Or different?

Finally, re-introduce yourselves as 1. your normal self. And 2. your essence art experience—and flow between.

Demonstration: I help and support CA and C to do this.

Amy: (Reading the exercise) Discuss possible shyness, discomfort, and possible problems together, and note rank differences with each other.

C: I asked CA to work with me.

CA: C and I have had differences around the white privilege groups. C is a big sponsor of that and I have been a detractor of organizing things around white privilege. I am not a big fan.

C: I want to clarify that. It is white people working on race issues and racism, not just white privilege. Working on our issues around racism, and white privilege is one part.

CA: I have not felt it is good to have white people meeting separately, working on racism. That has gone on too much, for too long.

C: I absolutely think we have a long way to go, we need to sit together and really work on our own challenges, embarrassment, edges. There are hard things, there. And I think it is important that we work together, get to know one another, speaking about people of color. There is a lot of segregation. A lot of white people grow up never relating to, and don't know, people of color. I think there is a time and place where we need to work together, to become more conscious.

Arny: What do you think, CA?

CA: I think it has gone on too long—in our community, particularly. It creates this "belonging" to a group, so you meet with those people. It creates difficulty. I am not into categorizing by groups like that.

Arny: Two viewpoints. Are there rank differences between you?

C: There is a friendship, where I don't feel a lot of rank differences. In your role of CEO, we talked about many things along the way, and I felt the rank differences, there. I felt not always able to stand long enough in what I thought, or felt, or expressed. I would give up a lot. I noticed I would feel depressed and drop down to a sense of not being able to stay. I often felt unable to access my power.

CA: I felt, as CEO, it was hard to be direct. I was held back by being CEO. Also, there were a lot of people interested in working in separate groups. I felt that many people were not interested in my viewpoint.

Arny: So, there is clarity about your viewpoints. Now, each alone, notice any possible double signals you make when discussing this problem. Notice any body feeling expressing something that has not yet been said.

CA: When you C, were telling me about your viewpoint, I felt you were teaching me. And part of me, perhaps appearing in a double signal, wanted to go like this [Holds his hand up against C].

Arny: That double signal shows resistance coming out.

C: I noticed that my head was very subtly nodding, looking like "yes," but I often had a "no" that does not come out clearly.

Arny: You guys are great. CA is saying, "No" and C's not much different.

CA: It is true. I am showing a yes, but saying no. Cranky. Underground. Withdrawing.

Arny: Thank you both, for being explicit.

Amy: Now, both of you relax. . . . Try to relax, breathe, and drop into the essence, as if you are a fish into the sea. Breathe, move, feel, and imagine swimming in the water and the waves. Feel the fish's relationship to the sea. . . . After a minute, explore how your Fish-Wave-Essence-Nature movement experience might be behind your double signals. Note and sketch that essence feeling. Make a sketch of this experience of being wave-like, of being moved. . . . When both are ready, one after the other, briefly share the essence experience beneath your double signal and a relationship message coming from that essence or quantum realm.

CA: Mine was like the ocean. It is so big and we are a couple of big fish, and are sitting there being moved by the waves and drinking beer. We are talking about the white privilege group. That is a great group! And the nonwhite privilege group—that is a great group, too.

Arny: Two fish drinking beer. I don't think I have heard that, before.

C: [giggles] In my experience, we were in the eddy of the river and we were like clown fish—with really big eyes. As fish, we are circling—waves are moving us in a circle, but we remain in eye contact, trying to really listen to each other and see each other. We are going back and forth, really committed to hanging out in this eddy till we felt like we could really understand each other. What was powerful about that was I had an insight—this is what needs to happen in groups. Whether we are all white, mixed, or people of color, we need to listen, to hear each other. You and I were not understanding each other yet. We have to hang out more, till we really hear each other. . . . The waves of the river made me feel like I could hang out with you, CA, till I can really feel you.

Arny: There is something shared there. Each of you has their own imagery, yet you both have a common ground of being and listening to one another.

C: Yes, our commonality and deeper dreaming is actually very similar.

CA: I am still studying it in myself, but something about the vastness of the ocean made it possible to just enjoy the larger mind. Sitting in this vast ocean, being rocked by the vast ocean, made it possible to realize C is part of a big ocean, and just relax.

Amy: Finally, reintroduce yourself as 1, your normal self, and as 2, your essence art experience, and flow between them.

C: My name is C. I am a strong activist around racial justice, and sometimes I want you to hear me more and understand. I see you trying. [laughs!]

CA: [laughter!] I really want to understand your point of view, and what you think and feel, and stay open—it is really easy in the eddy, letting the water move us.

[They both move, swaying, back and forth on the chairs]

Arny [to the class] They are dancing together. You two do not need to do much more.

CA: I like your clown fish, C, I like that, the big eyes in the big sea. I like it. It feels easier.

Arny: Your heads are moving close to one another and swinging a bit. Now you both look like waves, ready to have a longer conversation! Thank you, the two of you! Thank you for modeling the impossible.

[To the class] As onlookers, I hope you have a sense that there is an essence level to relationship that is beyond double signals, and that can be crucial in relating. They were very playful and expressive at that level, swimming in the water. I appreciate that.

[to C and CA] I never had a guru, but during your work, I thought of you two—as oh, great gurus, because what you did was a great relationship teaching.

After everyone does the exercise . . .

Arny: What discoveries did you make?

A: I worked with D, and it was amazing. I am Japanese, and he is Japanese American, and we realized we had something in common and we are also different. On the surface, we are constantly negotiating—are we connected, or different?

And on the essence level, we connect beyond nationality and ethnicity and felt closer. . . . We could have gone there through exploring double signals, but it would have taken much longer.

E: My process was being normal in consensus reality. Yet, from the essence level, things are not that important. It is a reflection to me, in my personal history, of how I can be a little rigid sometimes. . . . That rigidity is not all of me. . . . It was so relieving, refreshing, and rejuvenating to drop out and be moved. I really want to practice this the next time a problem spot arises. And I want to thank you for creating this exercise, for giving us practice for moving from phase 2 to phase 3, which is really the hardest place to get to on the planet.

Arny: Thanks. Remember, everyone, when we deal with the diversity issues, don't forget the quantum level and 2nd Training. There, we are flowing wave-like processes, connecting what appear to be separate parts and people in everyday reality. We need this wave state in order to avoid killing one another and to create sustainable multicultural communities. Be waves, and not just particles.

So, in brief, for all relationship problems, when you are blocked in communicating, remember the 2nd Training in relationships. Notice your double signals—things that you might feel shy about expressing to the other person. Then, drop to the essence, experience your breath, feel like you are a fish in the sea, and explore the feelings behind those signals. And share them with the other person. You might discover a new common ground world that can help you deal with personal and world problems.

PART V

Astral Dimensions of Body Symptom Work

• • •

THE 2ND TRAINING INTEGRATES DEEPEST psychological experiences connected with the quantum world, spiritual experience, and the universe.

Astronomical facts and metaphors, relativity, and some quantum thinking are introduced in the next two chapters to help with personal body problems and psychological issues.

We shall explore who we are in terms of the earth, the sun, and our universe; that is, in terms of geocentric, heliocentric, and noncentric universal viewpoints. There are down-to-earth body examples and 2nd Training exercises.

13. **Body Symptoms: Your Geocentric & Heliocentric Nature**

14. **Our Connection to the Noncentric Universe**

CHAPTER 13

Body Symptoms: Your Geocentric Heliocentric Nature

•   •   •

AFTER GRADUATING FROM THE JUNG Institute in Zurich, I was 30 and had pain in my foot—I could hardly walk. I had what was diagnosed as gout—too much uric acid in the blood, which piles up on your bones over time and hurts.

At that time, I had just become an analyst. I loved my teachers. However, they knew very little about psychology's connection to body experience. So, I researched psychology and medicine, followed my clients, and developed the concept of the Dreambody.[30] In short: all body symptoms mirror our dreams.

Still, I went to a standard medical doctor, as well. My doctor said, "You will have gout for the rest of your life. Gout never goes away."

I said to myself, "Ohhhh!" and wondered, "How can I extend the dreamwork I have learned?" From that question came what I called Dreambodywork. Its basic idea is that *what is happening to your body is mirrored in your dreams.* I will go into this mirroring later in this chapter, and go further, relating dreambodywork and dreams to our solar system.

Where Do We Live?

Most of us say we are from a certain spot or area on earth. But from a larger view, this earth is in a solar system. And our solar system's larger environment is the universe. So, the universe's dimensions are all part of our home, part of the reality that we do not often think about.

One of the reasons for connecting astronomy and physics to psychology is because I noticed that when I work with people around the world, as individuals and as part of large groups, most people seem shy to dream. Just about everyone splits off their personal identity from the whole of our planet, solar system, and universe.

Mainstreaming: We Are Geocentric

A common world problem is that we often center ourselves around our appearance, our group and/or the city we were born in. I call this kind of identity or centering "geocentric." That means, you measure your weight, size, color, and so forth and identify with some location or city. A geocentric question many of us ask ourselves is, "Am I normal or not, compared to others?" We compare bodies, minds, our racial and religious backgrounds and so forth to others, and often mainstream ourselves. Geocentric mainstreaming marginalizes dreaming, body feelings—and the rest of the world, solar system, and universe.

Universe?

Yes—perhaps you come from Mars! Did you know there are asteroids or small rocky bodies flying around in our solar system? Some might be rocks that flew off Mars, and banged into each other, creating asteroids that landed on the earth.

So, some of the molecules in your body may be Martian. Really! I am suggesting that it is OK to say you are from the earth; but parts of us are from Mars and the rest of the universe, as well. This is a fact, not fiction.

Don't marginalize where you feel you are from. You may have a certain appearance, and a certain color, and a certain behavior, and you might look like you are from a certain area on earth, but your more complete address is our solar system, our universe. So, focusing geocentrically only on the earth is normal, but is not sufficient to completely understand and appreciate yourself.

GEOCENTRIC MEDICINE

What would you say to me if I was one of the many people I work with who says, "I have a headache?" A medical suggestion might be to take an aspirin. But in processwork, (depending upon the person and their nature), we might suggest amplifying the headache feeling and the possible motion of that feeling. For example, if I had that headache, I might pound, or push, and to my surprise, I might feel stronger. This reminds me of a woman I worked with who pounded, found power, and went into politics to use that headache energy. Her headaches mysteriously got better.

MEDICAL DIAGNOSES AND ABUSE

Being geocentric means we mainstream ourselves and ignore dreams and the universe. When someone says to you, "If you don't feel well, go to your doctor and get help," the idea is that you are sick.

But consider and feel what happens to you when someone says, "You are sick!"

"Fuck you!"

Why do you say, "Fuck you!" when I tell you that you are sick? "Don't put me down! Fuck you!"

The medical community, as well as the geocentric world, look at you as SICK, which for many, can feel abusive. When we get diagnoses, whether mild or severe, it often re-constellates abuse issues. "You are sick! You are weird!" That hurts. Ever experienced something like that? "Sick is bad. Normal is good!"

Diagnosis often reactivates abuse issues and can create painful inner diversity issues inside of you. "You are not normal!" Of course, pathologizing can be important to help you find medicine and feel better. But the idea that you are sick marginalizes dreaming and any potential meaningfulness of your symptoms. Illness can become both a personal and social issue. I am discussing it now to help all of us, the medical community and the world, wake up to their geocentric, anti-dreaming viewpoints.

Geocentric means that the earth and our everyday human reality is the center of all things, the universe included. Many peoples, especially Eurocentric people, have always thought the earth was the center of the universe. Being geocentric, many didn't realize that the earth is *not* the center of our universe.

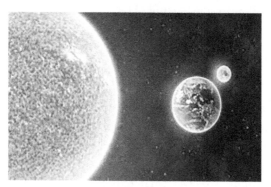

30. Sun, Earth, Moon

DREAM, LIGHT, AND SUN CENTERED

Being centered on the earth, we can ignore the dreaming and the power of the sun—as well as the rest of the universe. (Thanks, NASA, for the sun picture with the earth and moon in the background).

The early belief that the earth was the center of the cosmos was a mistake. Accepting the surface of the earth as their main reality is what European people believed for at least 2000 or 3000 years.

Early astronomers thought planets orbited the earth. People thought the earth was the center of the universe because when we watch the sun rise, it seems that the sun is moving around us on earth. We imagine being the center of everything and that everything circles around us. This incorrect astronomical idea was believed in the West until about 1500.

MODERN ASTRONOMY, BRIEFLY

Historically, around 1500, Copernicus (picture top right) noticed that the *earth was not the center of the universe.* It was not even the center of the solar system! He said that the sun is more central.[31]

31. Copernicus

The earth circles the sun!

The church at that time put him in jail for thinking that! Why? The church felt that God put people on earth, so the earth must be central. They felt hurt and turned against Copernicus and confined him.

Nevertheless, 100 years after Copernicus, Johannes Kepler (picture lower right) concluded that planets *really do revolve around the sun* and he found a mathematical formula to describe that.[32]

Now, the sun became the center of the universe, at least, for science.

What is the center of my universe?

If my normal geocentric mind is not the center, I must look for the center elsewhere. If the earth was the center, I would normally look only there. If the sun is the center, I must center myself around the sun and its light that gives me light. Enlightenment can come

32. Kepler

from many places, but dreaming, as I pointed out earlier in this book, is one of our main "lights." Dreaming is more central than our everyday mind; more central than the diagnosis of body issues.

THE MEANING AND LIGHT OF A SYMPTOM

A chronic or life-threatening symptom tries to knock out our consensus reality mind and reminds us that the sunlight of dreaming is central. *A chronic symptom that you cannot get rid of might be a gift, a kind of light to awaken you and detach you from your normal geocentric consensus reality self.*

Most of us will probably die within 120 years. But perhaps the fear of demise is based mostly on our geocentric consensus reality. If someone says, "Oh, my God! I have just got this terrible diagnosis"—don't forget it is possibly a gift, to awaken them to their sun: their dreaming center. The center of your life is the dream you had last night and the dreaming process behind each and every one of your symptoms!

YOUR LIGHT

The light is close to the idea of the gods. So, dreaming, the sun, and divine things are linked. Kepler led us to believe we are not geo- but helio-centric. Also, when I say that dreaming is central, that means not just dreams you had last night, but also your spontaneous, dream-like double signals and body symptoms. Your symptoms and double signals are all dreams: signals with an amazing potential light.

YOU ARE ALWAYS DREAMING

Symptoms and double signals are dream lights. My point is that being only realistic and geocentric irritates your body and provokes or even creates symptoms. In a way, there is no such thing as illness. You are just having another dream. Of course, if you don't feel well, take care of yourself in a more conventional manner—but don't forget your body's dreaming. Now, let us practice all of this with an easy exercise.

EXERCISE: HELIOCENTRIC DREAMBODY WORK

1. What repetitive body problem—X—bothers u most these days?

2. Feel + describe X's energy. Show X's dreamlike-imaginary behavior + energy.

3. What is your normal u energy like? Record + sketch these u + X energies.

4. What geocentric or normal solutions (if any) do you have for X? Have you tried using these solutions?

5. Explore #1: that is, ignoring X in consensus reality. Then #2: fighting X with accepted geocentric or medical solutions (if any).

6. In #3, use your (heliocentric) dreaming to experience + illuminate X's energy. Be helio- (sun-) or *dream-centered* and explore enacting X and role-switching between u + X. Record insights.

7. Finally, recall any possible geocentric medical solutions. Recall your heliocentric DREAM-like X + u experience. What's the difference, for you, between geo- + helio- centering? Make notes.

Demonstration of the exercise with K.

Amy: [Reading this to K] Do you have a repetitive body problem, X, that bothers you most these days?

K: Yes, I have a problem with my belly. I didn't think I would work on this [laughs!] . . . It has a lot of air, and is bloated—it is so uncomfortable! And the older I am, my digestion gets slower, and it feels more uncomfortable.

Amy: Digestion is slower—what is that like? I don't know what that is like.

K: I don't eat a lot—I don't eat much, but I have this feeling of bloating, air in the belly, and discomfort. 15 years ago, there was nothing wrong. . . . Today, when I am at work, I have to repress this feeling to get through the day, but it is awful.

Amy: If you could create that X bloating feeling and amplify it, what would it be like?

K: [shows arms extending in a big circle in front of her, hands clasped] It is big and static. [Holds the position] It is growing, expanding, expanding, but contained. There is something there, holding on.

Arny: Something is in there, filling you with air and holding steady.

K: Yes. I could do this more, but I cannot, because it is limited by my skin. My belly cannot expand more! . . . Having a body stops it.

Amy: What is your normal u energy like?

K: When you ask about my normal self, I see myself 20 years ago: light and effortless. That was normal, then! Freer!

Arny: Yes, your normal self, 20 years ago had no problem. We could walk around and do anything and have a good time without this weird stomach problem.

K: Yeah!

Arny: You are 20 years older. Are you aging?

K: Yes! I never thought it would happen to me!

Arny: No one plans on aging when they are 18 or 20. How old are you?

K: Ummm . . .

Arny: Don't say. It is a big thing. I can tell you how old I am! Shall I say? I am 79!

K: Wow!

Arny: How old are you?

K: OK, I am almost 40. [lots of laughter in the group]

Arny: Oh! Sexism and geocentric thinking play a huge thing. Being a woman is not always easy.

K: It is not so much internalized ageism . . . Well, I guess it is . . . I guess I wanted to do more things by the time I was 40 [starts to cry]. . . . So, in some way, it takes more time to work and it takes more time to do things. OK, so you are 79, but you were in Switzerland when you were 21, and your journey started earlier. I started my journey later. When Jung was 25, he was already known as a psychiatrist. Right? It takes so much time, so many human years to achieve something . . . and to live in a more effortless way [cries] . . . .

Arny: You are beginning life in some ways, wanting to come out and do things and this body thing may be stopping you, at least in your imagination. And that is agonizing.

K: For some people, it looks like I can do things fast, but it is just not fast enough . . . Of course, I am thinking now, "You are miserable. Everybody has a path. Don't compare yourself to anyone!" But from my subjective experience, life is painful. Shit! I hate this problem! Why didn't I do a PhD when I was 25?

Arny: OK, good geocentric questions. Now, let's go back to the symptom that is stopping you from going quickly ahead. How could you make that symptom happen to me?

K: [stands behind Arny, takes a moment to position herself, and puts her hands on his belly]

Arny: (Acting like K) I got to get ahead in life and do things!

K: [squeezes Arny's belly]

Arny: Oh! That X, what are you doing to me? Get the hell out of here! . . . I want to get busy! Give me some medicine! Call a doctor! Who are you? . . . I hate you! . . . Now I feel you pushing me. Pushing, pushing, pushing . . .

K: [Silent, as she pushes and tucks herself more under Arny's arm, almost carries Arny, her arms stretched out] Who am I? I am a silent being . . . It is kind of meditating, pushing, but very,

very slow . . . This slow feeling has the quality of *contained power*, and also the feeling of comfortableness about that. Exactly!

Arny: Let's say you really were this contained and powerful thing, at least for a minute.

K: No! No, Arny! What do I need to do?

Arny: I want you to go over your edge for a minute. Be the powerful, comfortable thing. Your secondary process looks like this power [pushes]. This is the quality of the energy [shows fists].

K: Yes! So, that is it!

Arny: You are five times more powerful than you think. Your primary process is shy about this power in front of the group, and the other part is Grrrrr!

K: . . . I am shy, from my Polish history . . . oppressed. Many people can't really get a better position or better job. But I want everyone to be more powerful . . . .

Arny: Your urge to be powerful is linked to geocentric, Polish, historical oppression, sexism, and more—but inside, you have all the power. . . . Behind that motion inside, behind the X in your stomach, is this power—not stopping you, but pushing you.

K: Ohhh! Thank you!! I got it!

Arny [to everyone]: If you really get deep enough into body work with somebody, you find world history. However, her symptoms want her to become powerful. Behind chronic symptoms are geocentric pieces of your history, social issues, historical issues. We are a piece of history trying to change. Symptoms can relate to huge social world issues. Yet the dreaming light, the power in the woman, appears as a symptom—in part, because that female power has been put down for centuries, in most cultures and groups. This is a big world issue.

After everyone does their body work . . .

Arny: How are you doing with your symptoms?

A: Feels better. My legs, less pain.

Arny: What was in there?

A: Polio . . . and it was not acceptable to be a cripple, so I made myself walk. In the exercise, I had a tantrum about being unacceptable and felt better afterwards.

Arny: Yes, you reacted to the geocentric opinions! And what came out of your legs?

A: A dance.

Arny: Can you show me some steps of the dance?

A: Really? [gets up and shows wild dance moves]

Arny: Yay! That dance is the right sunshine, the right medicine! You wiggle and move wonderfully.

Wow, we human beings are amazing and weird, aren't we? We are geocentric, but then free ourselves when dreaming, being more heliocentric. There are geocentric answers and then there are heliocentric dream-like answers. Don't center yourself only on earth. Remember the sun, remember dreaming. Remember your 2nd Training: center yourself sometimes geocentrically on earth, get frustrated, and then move fluidly in our process-oriented ever-changing mysterious universe.

CHAPTER 14

Our Connection to the Noncentric Universe

• • •

LET'S GO BACK ABOUT 13.8 billion—13 times one thousand million—years. Why? Aren't there enough problems today to work on? Yes, but perhaps we can find more solutions by exploring the beginning of the universe!

In the 2nd Training, we are most helpful to ourselves and our world if we connect not only to the city, country, and planet we live on, but also if we have contact with our solar system and the *entire* universe.

Astronomy is an ongoing research process, and nobody knows for certain how our universe began, or what its future will be. In the Big TOE I am suggesting in this book, the universe must be connected to our psychology (and spiritual traditions). So, astronomy and psychology are parts of the Big TOE. Remember, TOE means "theory of everything," including physics, spiritual traditions, and psychology.

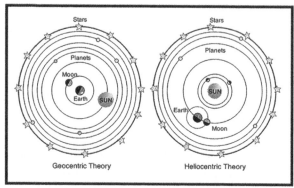

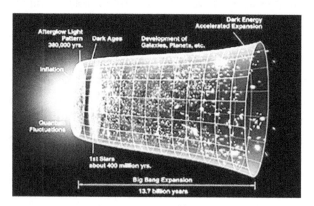

33. Universes and history

The pictures below will help us to understand the Big TOE. On the left, you see diagrams of the geocentric and the helio- or sun-centric universe. Then, in the middle picture, you see a picture of our Kenyan healer and some of her children. On the right, you see a picture of the history of our universe, of its expansion in the last 13.8 billion years, beginning with a bang from a huge area, not a single-pointed center. I will explain these pictures in greater detail as we move along.

As far as we know today, we live in a noncentric universe. Recall that 2000 years ago, most groups thought that the earth was the center of everything. Europeans had a *geocentric* theory, and *heliocentric* thinking began in the 16th century, with Copernicus and Kepler, in mainstream astronomy. The sun, not the earth, was then thought to be the center of our universe. Symbolically, this meant that light was the center. Psychologically, this can symbolize that everything that happens has light—or dreaming—at the center.

In the center picture, you see our friends, the witchdoctors from Mombasa, who asked us to take that picture of them. As I said in chapter 6, together with their whole tribe, they did a healing ceremony on Amy and on me. It was one of the most loving experiences imaginable. These beautiful people showed what it was like to create a unity—within themselves, with us, and their community. They welcomed us in, and said to us, "We baptize you. You are now African." They were amazing.

On the right, you see the history of our universe in brief. In 1924, the idea of a noncentric universe arose from the observations of Hubble, Herschel, and others. At that time, astronomers realized that the sun, although very close to the center of our solar system, was *not* the center of the universe at all. What was the center of the universe?

There is no one central point in our universe. Still today, almost 100 years later, no one knows exactly how our universe began.

Of course, research is ongoing. But imagine, if you can, that the known universe has no single-point center. Today's scientific data show that the universe began with the Big Bang 13.8 billion years ago—not at one point, as you can see in the picture, but from an area.

The Big Bang began when a huge extended piece of space exploded. If you are inquisitive, you might ask, "What was that space doing there in the first place?" Nobody knows the answer to that today. The theory of the universe is that it began with a Big Bang, but not from one point. The Big Bang happened everywhere in space at that time, with no known center. From measurements, we know the approximate time of the universe's beginning was 13.8 billion years ago.

Many of our psychologies have said that we must be centered. I love that, but there might be no one center for our universe.

The Big Bang illuminates processwork's essence level. Being central and having some central figure is part of modern psychology, but there is something else we need to consider as our "center": namely, the essence—which is not one point. The essence is a process experience.

Living on earth and being a realistic person on this earth means living in our solar system, and it also means *living in this universe. We are not just geocentric, living in* the here and now, but part of a huge, 13.8-billion-year-old ongoing process.

Remember, our center is not the earth, and not the sun. There is no one spot in space that was the center at the beginning of the universe.

The Big Bang suddenly expanded space, not from 1 point in space, but from a point in time. And it is still expanding now! As a matter of fact, it is now expanding even more rapidly than it did in the past. In the first several billion years, things were expanding at a fast rate, and more recently, in the last 2 or 3 billion years, the universe's expansion is accelerating: it is expanding even more rapidly, so that the velocity at which a distant galaxy is receding from us is continuously increasing with time.[33]

If you have questions about the universe, you are not the only one. Some physicists have speculated that there may be other parallel universes. However, up to now, those universes are not experimentally verified. All we know for sure is that our universe has spent about 13.8 billion years expanding—and recently, is expanding even more rapidly.

EXPANDING SPACE

The Big Bang happened in space, but not at one central point. There was no center. Let me demonstrate to you what I mean.

The concept of the universe means that somehow a huge dense piece of space appeared and exploded. Now, I want to just show what a noncentered expansion might look like.

Say Amy and I are standing together here in front of you. Now, if the space between us is expanding—we would move apart. Over millions of years, separation happens.

Now, if I bring in another person, and each of the three of us moves slowly and separately away from the other two, this is a noncentric expansion, as the universe is doing. There is a big, essence-like space in the middle, with more and more such space growing between us.

If we add a fourth person, and each of us inches away from the other three, relationship is still there. You can still love and hate; yet, at the same time, something else becomes as important or even more important, in any and all relationships. The basis or essence in relationships is *spaciousness*. You can still love and communicate with the others, but there is more distance, more empty space—a more relaxed, #4 empty mind in the middle that connects us now.

There is more distance or detachment in relationship. Closeness and the consensus reality difficulties are all terribly important. But I want to stress this whole spatial essence field that creates the possibility of distance. Having distance is a really important and missing quality in our personal and world psychology and conflicts.

Remember, our expansion is noncentric: there is no one center. Everything is expanding away from everything else, and in recent times, more rapidly than ever. The universe, our home, is just amazing.

The origins of the universe, and this expanding space we live in, remind me of the essence level's #4 detachment. Only when people get sick or depressed, have Alzheimer's, or are dying does some detachment occur. Needing distance, needing more space, is important. Otherwise, this need may come up as body experiences.

LONELINESS OR DETACHMENT?

Loneliness and isolation can be terrible killers if they are not integrated as essence-level detachment and quietness in relationship. This may be what the Buddhists and many peoples have been talking about for thousands of years. Have more distance, more creative detachment. This could create lots of fun, where there was just normal relating before.

When we are lonely, it is important to seek friendship. But with this essence level and the expansion of space, detachment and creative freedom may get people more friends, and more fun.

Out of the emptiness can come creativity. Remember our friend Fukushima Roshi, the head of the Rinzai sect in Japan? He said, "Empty mind is *creative mind*" because if you are totally empty, anything can pop out of you. You become very creative. In this space, there is potential creativity because the essence level is *empty mind,* or as the Roshi said, "*creative mind*"!

Our universe is a noncentric field. The Taoists might have called the space of our universe *The Tao that cannot be said.* This is a field power. There is gravity and electro-magnetism in there, and the power of essence experience. Expansion and gravity are important, but gaining distance is typical of our present universe.

If we are having an argument, after exchanging some words, there is a point at which either or both of us turn away. This turning away is not just due to depression or anger. Distance is an important signal. Among other things, increasing distance can signal more detachment. At the essence level in relationship—there is quiet, and there are deep feelings. The distance and quietness between us are very important and, in a way, paradoxically join us at the deepest levels.

When we are charged up in consensus reality, and we go away from one another, we are trying to get to that essence. Perhaps lots of break-ups are about finding a bit more detachment. This detachment can enrich the relationship, enabling it to function more fluidly. In other words, breaking up is metaphorically a way of getting to the essence level.

People think distance means isolation, but *spaciousness* means finally having space. Especially in the 2nd Training in relationships, the spaciousness of essence experience can make all kinds of parting and joining more fluid.

ASTRONOMY AND PROCESSWORK

Processwork's deep democracy levels are like astronomy. As I said in the last chapter, astronomy used to be earth-centered—geocentric—like today's consensus reality. "Let's focus on the measurable facts." Then, astronomy became sun-centered. For psychology, that can mean "be light-centered." So, let's dream more.

Processwork's essence level is symbolized in part by the noncentric expansion of the universe: that is, of space itself. Now, comes a very big question.

What is the meaning of being in a universe that is 13.8 billion years old? There is no one answer to that. But let's do some quick mathematics and squeeze 13.8 billion down to a more manageable figure. Let's imagine the universe is 100 years old. Relative to that 100-year span, how long would you say that human life has been here?

- Half a minute?

- A few seconds?

- 0.25 of a second?

If I was a 100-year-old universe, the blink of my eye would be the period the human race has been here. We human beings have been here for about one quarter of a second, relative to a 100-year-old universe.

What does it mean to live on this earth as a human person, knowing that the human race has been here, relatively speaking, for only a blink of an eye?

It means that we are very, very small and young, and not the center of things, as we usually think. Our history is very short. This means we need more contact with the essence level, with the origins of our ancient and expanding universe in dealing with our world.

To really live on earth is to live in the solar system, in a universe, creating spacious emptiness, stressing the quiet essence part of yourself and all things. It's normal to ignore the essence level; but if you do ignore it, you might encourage a health issue, depression, fear of death, or memory loss—to force you to sense the universe.

GEROTRANSCENDANCE

There is a term called *gerotranscendence* that describes the phenomenon that occurs towards the end of life, when older people seem to be half here and half gone. Thanks to Susan Kocen, for pointing me in the direction of studying this state of being simultaneously here and not here. We all need more everyday gerotranscendence, typical of our expanding universe. I discovered that Swedish gerontologist, Lars Tornstam, developed his theory of gerotranscendence[34] over a period of two decades. "The core of the theory suggests that normal human aging includes a range of vital and commonly overlooked components. In brief . . . there is an increased feeling of affinity with past generations and a decreased interest in superfluous social interaction. There is also often a feeling of cosmic awareness, and a redefinition of time, space, life, and death.

The individual becomes less self-occupied and at the same time more selective in the choice of social and other activities.

The individual might also experience a decrease in interest in material things. Solitude becomes more attractive."

An important insight from all of this is: *don't wait till you are older to experience the benefits of our universe. Dream while awake.* Saying that you did not dream at night is a lie! It is not quite true. Why? Because this essence level space in the universe, this emptiness, this empty mind at the essence level, is always ready to dream. You can tap into it at any moment.

Being here on earth is being part of this huge thing. However, really being grounded means being in touch with the universe, with its emptiness, with its open and empty mind—the core of the 2nd Training.

Our individual experience of the essence is a momentary experience of the field effect around us. The essence, like space, is not really *your* essence: it is your experience of space within you, as well as between and around us.

Sometimes, the deepest relationship happens when we don't talk, but when we share the space. So, sitting in a garden, quietly observing it together is more intimate than talking . . . just sharing space.

If you learn only one thing from this chapter, remember that the universe is 13.8 billion years old and that we have been here for a blink of an eye. To be a realist on this earth means to be in touch with that vast power and the spaciousness of our expanding universe, and not to marginalize it.

ASTROPHYSICS AND THE 2ND TRAINING

Being in touch with the universe's expanding space while also doing things on earth is another aspect of 2nd Training. Try the following exercise to learn more.

EXERCISE: HOW YOUR BODY EXPERIENCE CHANGES THE WORLD

1. Act out your normal u energy, and the worst fear you have about aging, grey hair, and dying—from some real or imagined body problem's X energy.

2. What can be done to stop that X? Now, feel, be moved, act out, and exaggerate that aging-dying X energy as feeling-movement, until it produces images and sounds, so you understand its message.

3. How do u need that message in your present everyday life? Make notes.

4. Consider how that body X energy might be a gift from the noncentric universe to remind you of your flowing

detachment in geocentric life. How would that X experience possibly change you and the world?

After the exercise . . .

R: So, I worked on the fear of dying. What happened was [laughs!] some imaginary loudspeaker came into my brain—and suddenly I heard it say, "YOU ARE ALONE!" It kept going, "YOU ARE ALONE!" and it upset me. So, then I imagined telling people, "You will now do inner work, alone. Everybody will now take 3-hour recess . . . and . . . PLAY!"

Arny: In other words, you are a world teacher of play. Loudspeakers are not for one or two people—they are about a world task.

R: Right.

Arny: And there is no such thing as being alone, there. You need to speak loudly to the world, "Now I am the boss! Let's play!"

R: Yes. You WILL NOW PLAY! GO TO THE AUDITORIUM AND PLAY!

Arny: Thank you, master! [lots of laughter]

K: My fear was also being alone, and the fear was poverty—dying under a bush, of tuberculosis, in the rain . . . And I cried and cried. As I came out of the crying, everything looked wonderful. Everything was bathed in this incredible state of wonder. It was a beautiful state and a deep appreciation of everything: the fabric, the textures, the leaves . . . an incredible state of wonder. Then, when my partner asked the question about how that will benefit the world, I said, "Wouldn't it be amazing if just for five minutes every morning, everybody woke up in a state of wonder? Just five minutes, noticing everything—and then get on with life, instead of that starving need for more—more ownership, more property, more money, more material things. We could see and appreciate with wonder what we have . . . I wish that for everyone, and for myself.

K: I was being crippled with pain—cancer. And I became the mud and the swamp, the slimy shit! But then, my hands came up from the swamp, and there was so much light and space, and I was very moved to bring the light and the space into the suffering. I ended up putting my arm around S, who was playing the suffering. I feel like the most ordinary mainstream person you have ever met, so it was kind of like a flip for me into that 2nd Training essence level "bringer of light"!

Arny: Yes, that is the flip I was looking for. You are a spiritual healer acting like a normal person.

Q: It is embarrassing to say what I was afraid of. It was looking in the mirror and seeing wrinkles! Then, that shifted so quickly.

Arny: How could that ever shift?

Q: When I was on the ground, I said, energetically, "I am dead, anyway, so why worry about it?" I was quite surprised by that. Worry was holding me back, but since I thought, "You are dead already, step into it!" I was surprised by the energy of the experience. It was a very energetic yang energy—not at all quiet and subdued.

Arny: When your ordinary self is reduced, and you die or come close to the essence level, you look so well and energetic! That's the 2nd Training in a nutshell! Enjoy the stars while on earth!

PART VI

Why Were You Born?

• • •

**Let's Find Your
Deepest Dream
and True Spirit
To Help Yourself
and Our Troubled World**

HELPING YOURSELF AND THE WORLD works best when you sense why you were born, and recognize your most basic patterns.

I realized from world-wide practical experience with thousands of people, including world leaders and world tensions, that everyone has their own specific *Healer + Leadership patterns.*

Yet, most of us are unaware of these crucial patterns. Therefore, we seek, find, and explore those patterns to answer deep questions, such as: Why were you born? What is your most creative leadership power?

15. **Who Are You? Why Were You Born? Patterns of Your True Nature**

16. **Your Leadership Pattern for Personal and World Relations**

17. **2nd Training Global Leadership Miracles in Reality**

CHAPTER 15

Who Are You?
Why Were You
Born? Patterns of
Your True Nature

. . .

REMEMBER THAT BEING REALISTIC AND having your feet on the ground means noticing that we live on earth in a solar system, and that our solar system is part of an immense universe. Follow your sense of that 13.8 billion year-old universe to detach and use your 2nd Training freedom to work best on earth.

Now, let's explore your particular, individual pattern: a part of your true nature that does not change much, in time. Why explore that nature? Knowing this will help you to realize the possible reasons WHY YOU WERE BORN. I have learned that if you know these things, your personal and worldwork will improve.

Were You an Accident?

Many think they are an accident that occurred when two people got together. In any case, accident or not, the question remains: who are you? If you know this, you can then use your *specific* patterns to help yourself and the world.

Your 2nd Training eldership will be deepened by knowing why you are on earth. There are too few elders in the world, helping with individual problems and world events, diversity issues, and world conflicts. Right now, there are too few elders, in part, because we are not taught how to connect to our deepest selves. Also, there are too few who know their particular gifts and patterns.

To help with your eldership and 2nd Training development, I will not only ask why you were born, but also *what are the most basic patterns guiding your life?* Knowing the answer to these questions will help to create a better life for yourself and a better world for all.

I will show how all of us were born with leadership and healer patterns. Those patterns and their use will be the focus of chapters 15, 16, and 17. One of the reasons for all our world problems is because *me* and *you* are not in touch with our own basic patterns to help us with the 2nd Training.

Religions suggest we need the gods to connect with our deep natures. I think of the best known world religions today—Christianity, Islam, Chinese Traditional, Judaism, Shinto, Buddhism, Hinduism, among others. All religions have ways of relating to the infinite, or what I have been calling the #4 experience.

I think, for example, of Jesus. In the Bible's Matthew 4, Jesus said, "Love your enemies." *Now, very few people seem to love their enemies.* That love would enable us to have the phase 3 experience of role-switching and the ability to look at ourselves from the other's viewpoint. This experience can lead to feeling for, or even loving, the X. But this experience is rare, and far from most people's awareness.

We are not usually aware of role-switching—except when you go to sleep at night and dream about the person you are against. Then, if you work on yourself in everyday reality, you might take your side and also experience their world from their side, as well. That sometimes happens in dreamwork—but otherwise, not often.

Why are we normally cut off from this phase 3? One reason is that we need to fight more, in phase 2. Take a stand and get important points across! Then, many years later, a few people can feel into the other side.

However, instead of dreaming and role-switching, we often create rules and laws. Loving the X becomes a kind of dream.

Nevertheless, everyone senses #3 and #4—and not only at night. How do I know? I did an experiment on the Oregon coast. I watched people as they looked at the sea. Just about everybody, from the age of 3 to 110, was fascinated by the waves, and said, "Wow!" They saw huge clouds of spray emerge from the wild Pacific Ocean and cried, "My God!" They watched the sunset in awe, and exclaimed, "Oh, my God!"

34. Newport Beach, CA (Thanks to Daily Mail)

I gently connected with those people watching the sea and asked, "What do you experience out there?" Just about everybody said, "WOW! Nature! The sky! The universe is awesome!" Some said, "God." One man even said to me, "I am going to build my church right here, looking out to sea."

In other words, I think everyone senses and believes in something infinite in nature. Each has their own way of naming it: Nature, God . . . and so forth.

If you belong to a religion, that belief system is important to you—wonderful. But everyone senses that amazing phase 4 experience of god or divinity.

#4 moves you unpredictably. But how you move is predictable! Your basic movement patterns repeat themselves again and again, over your lifetime. I will soon show you how you can see your typical patterns in the first dreams and fantasies you remember in life.

Before going further, I want to thank C.G. Jung! He gave a seminar at the University of Zurich in the 1st part of the last century. His course was called *Kinder Traume*[35] or Childhood Dreams. He said he could sometimes see, in those dreams, the future professions people would choose. I am not completely sure he is right about that, but the idea of childhood dreams patterning phases of your life seems very right.

Thank you, C.G. I feel him here, now, as I write. I hear him say, "That is enough! Get on with your work. You don't have to thank me anymore!"

OK. I have found that these childhood dreams and first memories pattern a great deal of what happens to us, beyond our possible professions. They may even pattern what happens near death.

In other words, I suggest that you will probably experience, again and again, what you have already experienced in the beginning—and throughout life. I think of Peter, with whom Amy and I worked and about whom I speak in my *Coma* book.[36]

His first dream or memory in life was about his sisters. In that dream, he was in bed in the morning, and his two sisters came on each side of him, hugging and holding him and each other.

That is exactly what happened to him, spontaneously, at the very end of his life. His wife and Amy, standing on opposite sides of his bed, were holding each other's hands, leaning across his bed as he was dying.

I have seen this kind of repetitive dream pattern occur many times, near death. Perhaps we are not just people, but timeless dream-like patterns. Remain open to the idea that you were born to carry such a pattern. Perhaps you are born to carry these first memories and patterns.

Think about a 1st dream or memory you can remember, just now, and write it down.

Now try this inner work.

1. Meditate and focus on the most impossible part of your first dream or memory. Think about, and feel the energy of the most problematic or troublesome part you experienced in those early years. Have you lived or integrated that energy in your life? Can you feel the energy of that troublesome part? It might be a little scary to meditate on that part. It might have been a spider, or a negative figure. It could have been a scary light or shadow.

2. How has that part appeared in your life, again and again? How has it moved you?

3. How have the more positive parts, and the negative parts of that dream appeared in your life up to now?

4. Finally, consider the possibility that maybe you were born to manifest these parts and powers, to bring them to consciousness.

I just want to suggest that perhaps you were born to manifest those dream parts and their basic patterns.

AMY'S CHILDHOOD DREAM AND PATTERN

For example, here is Amy's first dream or memory.

In the first dream I remember, I was about 5-years-old. In the dream, it was night-time, and I was in the basement of my father's warehouse—he had a furniture store. I was running, because there were these three Mafia guys running after me with guns, to get me. I kept running and got to an elevator.

Then, there were three different endings in this repetitive dream. One was that the elevator never came: that was a bad solution. Then, the second solution ending was that the elevator came, I got in and went up and was safe. And the last solution, on another night, was that they got in with me and we all went up together.

35. Amy's childhood dream:
Amy, the elevator, the Mafia

Arny: Now, if you think about those *bad guys,* how have these troublesome figures appeared in your life?

Amy: Like many people, I have an inner Mafia-like critic who is always after me. Sometimes, I experience them as people in the real outer world, as well. But then, when I integrate their tough energy, I feel that there is a lot of definitiveness and real power coming out of me.

Arny: When you use the power of what looks like a critic—when you pick up its power—it changes. Perhaps Amy was born, in part, to help these apparently negative powers become elevated and use them in an elevated or spiritual way. I mean, HER way.

Perhaps one of the reasons we are born is to bring these early patterns to consciousness, for ourselves and for the world around us. Make these childhood patterns conscious. The world needs you.

Perhaps we are dreamlike waves. Remember quantum physics: before a particle is viewed, it is a wave-form. Then, when it is observed, it appears as a particle. In the same way, perhaps we are wave-like dream patterns. When the universe or world looks for something like you, it dreams you up as your wave nature becomes images, parts—like particles.

Perhaps the world is looking for you and your childhood dream patterns. From this viewpoint, you are needed in this world. You are not just accidental or meaningless. The world needs you to become conscious of your different parts and bring them out.

K: I was so touched to hear my parents share their dreams. It changed everything for me and my relationship with them. I thought my father would tell me to shut up, tell me I was too psychological, but he didn't. When I asked him if he had an earliest memory, he answered, instantly, "Romek." So, I said, "Romek, what is that?" And he looked at me and said, "That is the diminutive of my first name, Roman." His first memory was being a very little and beloved child. It was very touching to feel that "Romek" part of him.

Arny: That is a good example of a childhood memory or first dream.

K: My father survived the Holocaust in Poland.

Arny: in a concentration camp?

K: He was a boy in the Warsaw Ghetto, he was smuggled out and then hidden for three years.

Arny: Perhaps that dream figure, the child Romek, helped him to survive that difficult world at that time. Perhaps inside that childlike energy was the adorable power to survive all that suffering.

Now, let's work with the childhood dream energies.

WHY WERE YOU BORN? YOUR CHILDHOOD DREAM OR 1ST MEMORY

This exercise is inner work to rediscover yourself. You will need paper and something to write with. If you track your experiences on paper, you will be able to use them later.

The dream might resolve some of your worst long-term problems. Again, do record the earliest dream you remember or your earliest memory. It could be a dream or a first memory. I would choose the dream if you have a choice, although they are both good.

We shall be focusing on a couple of the energies of your childhood dream, and then we are going to be asking you about a long-term problem you have had, a recurring problem. Then, we will ask about the most difficult energy of that problem—the X energy.

Demonstration with Arny.

Amy: Did you have a childhood dream that you can share?

Arny: In my dream, I was fixing or cleaning my father's car. I will sketch it. I was fixing or cleaning it, and a bear appeared. The bear chased me away from that car and into ever-larger circles. I went back into the car, and the bear said, "No!" and pushed me out again into bigger circles! The two or three central figures were me, the bear, and the car. *Amy*: Can you feel and act out the energy of those three?

Arny: [plays the car, making engine noises]

Amy: And the bear?

Arny: Grrrrr! And as the bear, I sleep a lot, and when I wake up— Ha, ha, ha! Let me chase Arny out of that car and into ever greater circles.

Amy: Are you aware of how any of these figures or energies have been present in your childhood experiences?

36. Arny's childhood dream images (sketch by Amy)

Arny: Yes, I always liked fixing things, physics and engineering. And in the dream, I was fixing my father's mechanical car, even though I was only 3 or 4 years old. My parents were always asking me to fix household things, even when I was very little.

Amy: Like what?

Arny: Electrical circuit problems!

Amy: OK. So, your engineering knowledge was present, even then.

Arny: Apparently. I was always interested in how real things work. In any case, big energies came up against me from the outside world as I began school. Older children approached me on the street and said they wanted to kill me. They said, "You are a part of the wrong religion and you have to die!" and they tried to kill me. It took me years to fight back and finally befriend them. . . . I felt chased, for years afterwards. I am still nervous about going down certain dark street areas at night. . . .

That old scene looks bad, but today, I am thankful for it. Because if it was not for those kids in 1945, as World War II was ending, I would not have been forced to think about world issues and develop worldwork. They helped me to become a more multicultural person. It is a long story, but that is basically it. I don't want to go into the details, now. Let's say they drove me out and into the world. I am thankful for that. I learned how to fight, and years later in high school, I began to love them—and they voted me in as their class president.

Amy: Why do you love them?

Arny: Because I totally understand them and their feelings, and because, together—we are the world. Thanks to the dream and the bear energy for forcing me to make greater circles beyond my personal identities.

Amy: OK. Now, let me ask—how much time do you spend in different phases? How much time do you spend in phase 1, being happy, just thinking about things?

Arny: Oh, about 20%, although this all depends upon the day.

Amy: Phase 2, being in conflict, tension, and all of that?

Arny: Well, phase 1 is boring, so I turn to the world issues that are always asking for help, or personal inner work issues, so I focus on phase 2 a lot of the time.

Amy: How much time do you feel you spend in phase 3, dreams? Dreaming into this or that?

Arny: I have always done that quite a bit, even as a child. Maybe 25% of the time. You know, I love dreaming and picking things up.

Amy: I think you do it more than that! But it is your work, here. I shouldn't say anything or evaluate you, but you do #3 a lot . . . And phase 4, the essence level, how much do you feel the universe moving you?

Arny: It comes and goes. Perhaps 10% of the time?

Amy: Can you name one of your long-term, recurring, personal inner tensions or problems?

Arny: I am about 79, heading toward 80, and get a bit more tired running than I did in the past.

Amy: I still can't keep up with you! So, what is the X energy of that problem?

Arny: Going downhill! I hear, "Arny, you are croaking!"

37. Going downhill

Amy: Can you act it out? Get a feeling for it. [Arny makes more sounds, "ooooo-!"]

Amy: Can you somehow make a sketch of that X energy?

Arny: That X energy? [draws a descending squiggle]

Amy: Is that energy somehow seen or implied in your childhood dream somewhere?

Arny: Yes. That energy, in my association, belongs with the car that I like fixing. [makes sounds of a car starting, turning over, and then running]. So, I am fixing the car.

Amy: And even though this energy seems negative or difficult, is there anything good about that car problem?

Arny: Yes. Tiredness . . . letting go . . . is beautiful! That is neither good nor bad, it just feels really well to let go. That frees me to dream and be more creative.

Amy: OK. So, now go into the phase 4 experience. Relax and we will drop things for a moment. Breathe, meditate, and just let yourself be moved.

Arny: [Arny goes inside, moves slowly and begins wiggly movements and a sudden energetic whoosh upwards occurs].

Amy: As you are moved, notice repetitive movements that occur, and possibly, images that go with them.

Arny: The image I have is letting go and then, this spontaneous, sudden energetic gesture upwards occurs.

Amy: Are those repetitive motions found in your childhood dream?

Arny: That is interesting. There is the automobile I am working on and the bear that comes and whooshes me out and away from the car. "Get out of there!" The bear comes and woofs!

me out in the world. That bear chases me out of the car. The energetic motion comes from the bear.

Amy: Can you make a little sketch, here? Of that motion, that movement experience.

Arny: It reminds me of my first sketch of the bear coming into the car as I was fixing it and making me run out into the world, and go "Woof!"

Amy: Does that movement experience give you any more insight into the dream, and maybe into that tiredness problem?

Arny: Yes, what I am calling aging is me fixing the car. The bear, however says, "GET OUT of THERE! Remember the dreaming body!" That is probably where my idea about the dreaming body came from. . . . I was thinking about the body problems years ago and the bear came to me then, and said, "Forget the car (body) and think about the dreaming body!"

Amy: Does it give you any more insight into the tiredness? Or insight into aging?

Arny: . . . . [ha!] Aging? Forget it! Remember the larger perspective, the dreaming part of your body, the bear! Not just the mechanical car!

Amy: Consider that the universe brought you to birth to live this dream and be spontaneously moved.

Arny: Yes, perhaps I am here to work with and let go of my everyday mind and be moved by that bear energy as much as possible.

Amy: Can you guess, looking at this dream and from your experience, what the universe wants from you now, in your life?

Arny: What it wants from me now in my life? . . . [is quiet, then makes wild motions again!] Make a bigger circle! . . . Make a big circle! Include as many people, as many countries, as many places as possible! Many peoples. Our one world in this universe. I don't like that there is so much pain in the world. I would like to make bigger circles to include everybody. . . . The bear says, "Get out there! Help the world!"

Amy: Thank you for doing that. All this reminds me that your work has gone from dreambody and relationship work to worldwork, and your recent books are going out towards the Universe and the cosmos. The circles are getting larger.

Arny: I want to bring together various spiritual traditions, different peoples, the universe, astrophysics . . . I want to see how big a circle we can make.

Amy: That is so touching. I feel that you are working in the middle on your own myth and some of us share aspects of that pattern. Interesting—next month, we will be flying in a very big circle around the whole globe to help various cities around the world.

Arny: Yes! I want to help others.

Let's all now try this inner work.

EXERCISE: WHY WERE YOU BORN?
(INNER WORK TO REDISCOVER YOURSELF)

1. Recall a childhood dream or 1st memory. Once again, notice/highlight or circle 2 or 3 of its central figures/ energies. Feel and act each of them out with your hands and possibly whole body, and then sketch and name them on paper. How were these figures or energies

present in your childhood experiences, somewhere? Make a note.

2. How much time do you generally spend in phase 1 + phase 2? That is, just wanting to relax or avoid problems, or in the midst of tensions and conflicts? Make a note. How much time do you focus on phase 3 dreams and dreaming, or on your phase 4 deepest experiences—on the essence level experience of being moved? Make a note.

3. Name one of your long-time, recurring, personal, or inner tensions/problems. Make a note. What is the most difficult inner figure or energy of that tension/problem? Act out that energy with your arms and whole body, and perhaps add sounds. Then, sketch and name that problem energy or figure.

4. Is this problem energy somehow implied or related to a figure, part, energy, or action of your 1st dream or memory? Make a note. Even though that troublesome X energy seems negative, what could possibly be good about it? Make a note.

5. Stand, if possible. Relax, breathe and meditate, and carefully be moved by the universe . . . (being careful of your body) . . . until spontaneous repetitive movements and images arise from those movements.

6. Are these movement-energies-experiences somehow pictured in your dream? How? Make a note about it and sketch the movement experience. Does this movement experience give you any new insights into your childhood dream/memory pattern and any new insights about the problem mentioned in number 3 of this exercise? Make notes.

7. Consider if perhaps the universe brought you to birth to live that dream and be spontaneously moved, as you just were. Try to guess, from that dream, what the universe wants of you now. Make notes and share your dream and insights with someone near you.

Keep asking and rediscovering, "Why was I born?"—because if you get a sense of why you were born, you will come closer to your own sense of life and your work in the world.

Perhaps we are dreamed up by a world that needs us as we are! Perhaps life is about making our basic patterns conscious.

The world, the universe, is looking for you. We need you, and your basic pattern. If you are conscious of it, chances are that you and those around you will be happier.

CHAPTER 16

Your Leadership Pattern for Personal and World Relations

. . .

YOUR CHILDHOOD DREAM AND/OR FIRST memory organizes the patterns you live by. Our planet needs you and your dream. Perhaps in some way you have been dreamed up by the world to bring your particular nature to consciousness and to help our world.

Knowing your childhood dream helps in relationships. Your first dream or memory organizes a lot of what occurs between you, your enemies, lovers, and friends. For example, recall that early childhood dream or memory. Recall the negative, more problematic energies or figures in that dream. Remember the parts looking more positive and those that look more negative.

Now, think of your first big relationship problem. Choose a difficult relationship. Later on in life, you might have had many relationships, but think of an early one that was troublesome.

Now, imagine how aspects of your childhood dream might have influenced and created that relationship. For example:

- What aspects of that childhood dream might have been important in creating that problematic relationship?

- What aspect of that childhood dream or memory might have been helpful if you had had more access to that aspect at the time? Make a note about that.

- Imagine using this helpful part of your dream in that relationship. What might you have done, if you had been more conscious of this helpful part? Do remember this aspect of your memory or childhood dream that could have helped.

Perhaps first dreams predicted problems and solutions in that early relationship. We will work on this later. At this point, consider that we create relationship problems and can also create relationship solutions.

I can give you an example of my own. My childhood dream was about taking care of my father's car, and a bear came and chased me away and around in ever-larger circles. I think about my first marriage. In that first problematic relationship at the age of 21, I was more identified with the father, with wanting to be a typical, standard family person. Have a car and a family!

But the bear did not agree. He chased me out into larger circles. Eventually, that relationship problem got resolved, but if I had been smart enough at the time, I would have said, "I identify as a family person living in one place, but there is another part of me who identifies with the larger circles around our world."

Early on, I could have appreciated my partner at that time, and then said, later on, "I have a different pattern." Later I married Amy, who loves being at home but also works with me traveling all around the globe 32 or more times.

Identifying with only one part of the childhood dream or memory is natural, but that identification can create problems. We are *all* of the parts and relationship potentials in our childhood dream and memory. Your larger pattern can help you to be more conscious in relationships. For example, if I had known better in my first troublesome relationship, I would have been a more typical family man, and more consciously interested in creating larger circles or families around our world.

A good relationship is based on people matching all of the energies in their childhood dream patterns. If you are identifying with only some of the energies, that is normal. But the best relationships are ones in which you can live ALL your different dream patterns, and are matched at least in part, by the other person or people.

Now think of a second problematic relationship you have had at some time in your life. How were difficult moments *there* prefigured by your childhood pattern?

Remember process, or phases, in relationships. We will be working on this, but I would like you to embrace your relationship pattern as well as its phases. Relationship patterns involve phase 1, ignoring problems: "let's relax!" In phase 2 there is tension: "We can't avoid that!" Conflict is a phase, but remember that in phase 3, *you are a bit like the other person. So, remember to take their side.* Step into their shoes and speak for them. This may lead to the phase 4 aspect of relationship: the sense of peace and centeredness.

Especially in relationships phase 2, remember rank and diversity issues. Both of you, or all of your partners, must deal with diversity issues around gender (remember sexism), race, sexual orientation, age, nationality, religion, and health issues.

Mainstreaming in relationships occurs when you think, "I should look normal. I should act/be like some standard, mainstream person." Remember, mainstreaming is the pressure to conform to a particular type of mainstream group—which might be very different from the way you really are, look, or feel. The person who is being mainstreamed most is often in pain and asking for understanding, even if they are not saying it verbally. That needs to be taken into consideration in relationship—otherwise mainstreaming pain prevents fluidity in relationships.

Many of us have been mainstreamed away from our childhood dream pattern by socialization. All of us suffer—at least in part—from socialization.

Remember, mainstreaming in relationships makes us forget our own feelings, movements and phases in order to act like others. In relationship conflict, phase 2—Grrr!—is normal, but remember to use phase 3, where you can switch roles. Phase 4 always appears as a detached experience that will allow you to notice little things that flirt with your attention. So, don't forget to have a meditative #4 attitude, also, in relationship work. That belongs to the 2nd Training and can make relationships more fun.

Recall your phase 4 spontaneity. I recall the Roshi, about whom I have spoken many times before. The reason I loved that guy was because of his freedom from normal relationship ideas. When we went to visit him in his monastery in Kyoto, Japan, everybody was bowing to him. But I just could not do it. My favorite gurus have always been my best friends, and so I went over to him with my arms open and he forgot all the bowing down, came over to me and we hugged. It was spontaneous.

One of his calligraphies says, "Don't think too much." He was always trying to focus on what we call phase 4 and what he called *no mind, empty mind, creative mind.* That is, *mu-shin.*

Mu-Shin

This Zen expression is sometimes referred to as the state of "no-mind." That is, a mind open to everything.

When the Roshi came to visit our house on the Oregon coast, Amy showed him a basket she made years ago, out of newspaper. She will tell you— she thought it was very cool.

**38. Fukushima Roshi
(Thanks Wikipedia)**

Amy: "I was completely full of myself; had no empty mind at all. I came up to him and said, 'Roshi! Look at my basket!' I was like a little child showing it to my parents. And he took it, went, 'Oh!' and put my basket on his head!"

#4, or being spontaneous in relationship, is a kind of relaxed, creative, and unpredictable action. We will be using that phase now in 2nd Training relationship work.

2nd Training Relationship Work

This meditation explores how your childhood dream energies could have been used with a past relationship issue. To flow with conflict situations, let go into your #4 experience and how that altered state helps. Then, your partner will again play an X, and you will let your #4, 2nd Training help.

Exercise: Your Personal Leadership in Relationships (inner work or dyad)

1. Who is/was your most difficult personal outer relationship? Choose one and make a note. What is or was that person's worst X energy that disturbed you? Act out

this X energy so your helper can play it for you later. Sketch and make a note about this X energy.

2. Tell your 1st dream, and act out the feelings and/or energies of 2 or 3 central figures in the dream. Now imagine using those childhood dream or memory's *energies to* relate to the difficult person *(acted out by the helper)* and their X energy. If needed, bring in the phases 1 (forget it all), 2 (conflict), or 3 (role-switching). Continue until something changes or you need more insight.

3. Then, relax, and in phase 4, let yourself be moved spontaneously by the universe (be careful of your body and others around you). Wait for repetitive motions and feelings and note these feelings and possible meanings. Those feelings and movements are your universe dance pattern.

4. When you are ready, continue to feel this spontaneous creative dance pattern. Imagine it, and use it to understand and/or relate best to the X *(still played by the helper)* and notice the effects. Partner, notice when you feel changed and give feedback about it. Make notes about your learning.

5. Finally, what did the experience you just had teach you about *your leadership ability* in relationships? Make notes about your learning and leadership ability.

WORLD LEADERSHIP

I think you were born to carry a certain kind of pattern, which you can see in your first dreams and experiences. This pattern can be helpful not only in personal work but in all relationship work—and in the world, as well.

You are gifted with a relationship pattern that our world needs. The more you know about that pattern and bring it out, the more you can help our world.

One of the biggest world problems is not the lack of world leaders, but that you do not see *yourself* as a world leader.

I hear you say, "Me? A world leader?"

Yes.

"What am I supposed to do?"

Live your particular pattern or process in whatever you do. If it is painting, use it there. If it is dancing, use it there. If it is teaching or government, use it there and everywhere. We need your pattern, for a better world.

We should have learned about our patterns in kindergarten, because this work is elementary. Even though thinking about the symbols might be new for some people, it is also simple. Perhaps some people have a dream-leadership style for life of sitting quietly and meditating. If they really meditate, if they really go inward in their own way, that will help the world.

In other words, world leaders are not just people who are out there, leading. Everyone who lives their own dream *helps the world. We need all of us to be our deepest self in all the things we do.*

WORK WITH WORLD LEADERS

We will do a triad exercise to bring your childhood energy to the work with world leaders. But first, let me give you an example of integrating this relationship work into the world, in everyday life. It is an example from worldwork.

At one point this winter, we were in the mountains near Bend, Oregon, skiing on Mt. Bachelor in Central Oregon. One morning, we drove up close to the mountaintop to go skiing.

When we were in the parking lot, putting on our skis and boots, we suddenly heard this person far away in the parking lot, screaming loudly. She was shouting at somebody. We ignored her at first, and continued putting on our ski equipment.

Although the screaming woman was far away in the parking lot, we could hear every word. She was yelling at another woman, "It is always about you! *You* wouldn't get in the car. *You* have been doing this all day! I cannot stand it! You always do the same thing!" She was screaming and screaming. "You are horrible! I hate you!"

Although she was at a distance, she was screaming so loudly everybody could hear her. She went on and on. And the other woman who was her enemy stood quietly, looking depressed, on the other side of the car with her head down, shoulders shrugged.

Amy thought, "Oh, God, what is happening? Those women will deal with it."

But Amy continues, "Then Arny, who was half-way done getting his ski boots on, said to me, 'Oh, great! I hope they'll still be there by the time I get there!' So, I scrambled to get my stuff on, and we skied over to them. The woman was still screaming at the top of her lungs and the other woman was cowering on the other side of the car.

"Arny got there, went right up to the angry woman and said, 'You are very strong and that is really good. That is wonderful . . . but don't forget that you love each other, and the other woman is very sensitive,' pointing to the quiet one.

"And you won't believe this! I had to write it down! The angry woman looked up and said in the sweetest voice to Arny, 'You are a very sweet man!'

"Meanwhile, I [Amy] went up to the one who was shy. I had no idea what to say, and I said, 'We all go through these things. I really understand.'

"Then, the one who had been angry said to Arny and me, 'You know, I wish I could ski, too, but I have osteoporosis, so I can't ski, and it is just really sad.' She suddenly became the weak one in the group. 'I wish I could go with you,' she said to us.

"So Arny said, 'You can ski a little bit. Your bones are troublesome, but you could carefully try it, at least a little bit.'

"She smiled and wanted to keep talking. But suddenly, Arny or his bear said, 'Goodbye! We are going skiing!' and we left to ski. We looked back, and you won't believe it. We saw the two women walking together, hand in hand, as they got in their car and drove off.

In this story, the mean woman switched, and became the weak one. And the other one looked better. It was a really good example of how we can apply this work to personal relationships, and then, to outer or world figures and situations.

Skiing can be fun. Amy tells me, "You are always going into these impossible situations! With your skis half on, you couldn't wait to get there! You do it all the time."

Where there is a problem, I want to go. Not forgetting Amy— or skiing!

World Figures

Let's now apply all this to working with world figures. One person will be the reader/guide, guiding through the exercise; one person is the person working in the exercise, and the other person will play the troublesome X figure being discussed. Here is the exercise.

EXERCISE: YOUR RELATIONSHIP LEADERSHIP PATTERN TO HELP OUR WORLD

(In triads—one person works, one is the reader, one will play the X)

1. Make a note about which world figure bothers you most. Feel, act out, and show this figure's worst X energy (so the third person will be able to play that X). Make a note about that X. Where do you meet that X somewhere in personal relationships? How (and when) are *you* like X in some way? ☺ Make notes.

2. Person working—recall, tell, feel, move and express two or more of your 1st dream figures or memory energies. Third person, now act out the world figure X. Then, person working, use your dream figure energies, as needed, to relate best to X, until something changes. Use your basic two or three childhood memory or dream energies to deal with the problem person X.

   Again, if you are the person playing the X figure, notice when something changes, even if it is very subtle. Don't keep going. Stop and say, "I notice that little thing you did really got to me and changed me." That is a key moment.

3. Then, when ready and needed, relax and let go, in phase 4. That is, let yourself be moved spontaneously by the universe. (Be careful of your own body and others around you.) Note various movement and feeling experiences and let ideas or tips arise spontaneously *about how to deal with the X*. Now, when ready, use those experiences as your 2nd Training to help you relate to X (still played by the 3rd person) until some understanding happens.

4. From this relationship experience, describe your *Relationship Leadership Pattern* to help the world. Write this down. And make a plan to share your insights and experiences from this relationship work with others in everyday life.

Why are we suggesting #4 dreaming? It is because when you are relaxed, and you just let yourself be moved, a particular movement arises again and again that you will probably be able to find in your childhood dream pattern. That fluid movement is central to your 2nd Training.

I want to appreciate each and every one of you, for working on personal relationships and world problems. If we all did that, the world would change for the better.

CHAPTER 17

2nd Training Global Leadership Miracles in Reality

• • •

PERHAPS OUR LEAST KNOWN AND WORST GLOBAL PROBLEM is that we are not aware of our own particular 2nd Training skills. As a result, we leave WORLD CHANGE to world leaders! So, let's focus on Global Leadership Miracles at everyone's edge.

When we arrived on this earth, we apparently came with a particular pattern that appears in early dreams and memories. Those dreams show that each of us has a unique way of moving through life and dealing with its challenges. The core of the 2nd Training is realizing your unique

39. On the wings of a dream

way, using your spontaneous processmind dance, to actualize the energies of childhood dream and memory figures.

I have been asking *why are you here?* Is there a reason for you to be here? My answer comes from your dreams. Yes—you are needed on earth to live those dreams. Not only your family but your culture and our whole world dream you up, so to speak. You are not just an accident. There is an apparent reason that you are here: to realize and use the power of your own specific pattern. The world needs your pattern.

We don't need one world leader. We need everyone to be a world leader to actually change the whole world.

Using quantum physics as a metaphor for explaining our appearance on earth, we might say that when you are needed and looked for, your potential (perhaps, wave-form) appears. When the world seeks you or a community needs you, your wave-like pattern is *viewed* and transforms into a particle (as in quantum physics). In brief: you were born.

When needed, the world dreams us to be here. It is very important to feel this, because it can make your life more meaningful. Yes, do your studies and any work you can do, have relationships, a family . . . or not . . . make a living and all the rest of it. But also remain open to the possibility that there is some special thing trying to manifest through you that our world needs.

World change depends not only on the big leaders—but also on you, me, and everyone. It depends on the way you are in school, at work, the way you are in a relationship. It depends upon you living your deepest self and basic patterns. If everybody realized their basic patterns, the necessary world changes would be easier.

We need you, *your* way, and *your* repetitive childhood dream pattern. Please love yourself by appreciating your own particular nature and the giftedness that you bring to the world with that pattern. How and when it manifests requires awareness: 2nd Training awareness. When you are in the middle of a tense situation—when you don't know what to do next—relax and follow your dreaming body. It uses your original dream energies for the benefit of all.

World change depends upon you, upon all of us. I know this

from my practice, from working with different leaders around the world. I have already mentioned my work in Switzerland. People would sneak into Switzerland to work on stuff, hoping they would not be seen doing that by the rest of the world. So, I saw leaders coming in and wondering about changes their countries needed. Just getting them to walk around and notice what motions came up was so helpful. Those things have led to social changes in their countries.

They had the power to enact their dreaming. But we need *you and everybody* to be able to enact *your dreaming* to really change our world. Those world leaders wanted to follow their dreaming, and with help, they tried and made helpful changes.

But we need everyone, for sustainable change! World change keys are inside you. Please appreciate the positive and apparently negative energies in yourself and use them as best you can. Each of us is a leader, each in their own ways. Be open, and center yourself in your childhood dream energies. Don't wait for so-called world leaders to change the world.

Because your childhood dream contains a message needed by the world, let's use that message right now. Think of a problem in your family, city, or your country. Now ask yourself: HOW could the energies of your childhood memory or childhood dream possibly influence or help the problem that you are thinking about—in that family, city, or country system? Don't forget to make a note about your answer.

We will be working more on this, shortly. I just wanted to warm you up for the meditation that will follow.

Try to sum up your childhood first memory, dream figures, and experience. For example, in my case, there is my father's car and a bear that is chasing me in ever larger circles. So, the summary for me would be to recall my father's good-hearted nature, and don't forget to follow the bear that presses me to make ever larger circles around the world.

See if you can sum up your childhood dream or memory in a simple manner. Write it down and put it in your wallet. If you ever get lost in life, just pull out your wallet and see what you wrote down.

Arthur Waley, translator of the *Tao Te Ching*—a fundamental text for both philosophical and religious Taoism—said all of this very simply. (I am using "She" instead of "He" here). That book says, quite simply:

"The Sage arrives without going. She sees all without looking. She does nothing, yet achieves everything."

How can a Sage arrive without going? That is what I am suggesting as a 2nd Training ability. She does nothing yet achieves everything. There is nothing wrong with sweating and pushing, but if you are really in touch with your processmind experience, it dances. Then, when you do things, you do nothing, so to speak— and all is done! Be in touch with your processmind and dreaming process.

Remember, when you feel tired and exhausted, your process wants to relax, so you can enact your 2nd Training. *Let your dreaming mind move you so that it does things. If you get tired of doing things, let not-doing happen.*

Following your processmind is a mixture of following your body, your basic 1st dream pattern, and being moved in great part by a universal or processmind energy we cannot explain. Taoists called this energy we cannot explain the "Tao that can't be said."[37] So, follow your processmind. It follows the Tao or unspeakable powers of the universe.

The early Taoists must have understood this central aspect of what I am calling the 2nd Training. They said that the Sage arrives without going or doing anything. I really love that. If you are in touch with yourself, things happen. I have not always been able to do that. It took me time to learn it. For example, when I was at the Jung Institute, years ago, I did not yet have a 2nd Training. I was an analyst at the institute and I went through the programs and became a Training Analyst. It surprised me when I began bodywork that conflicts arose around me because I was not sufficiently aware of myself.

I would work with people, but not just on their dreams. They would come to see me, and I would say, "Well, how is that dream connected with your body experience?" And we would start to work on body experiences and their dreams, and my dreambody idea arose. My clients and I got all excited about that.

Students at that Institute had to have several analysts. So, my clients would go to their other analysts and say, "Can you work on my body, too? I had all sorts of good experiences with Mindell."

You can imagine—the other analysts were not always happy. They said to the clients, "What are you talking about?"

The clients would say, "My body is dreaming. Don't you want to help with that, too?"

They would say, "Hmmm! I don't know about that Mindell! He is doing unknown things."

My own unconsciousness was the problem. I never intended to do anything new. I did not want to break away from anybody. I was not interested in any of that. Everything I did was part of dreaming—my bear who brought me into ever larger circles.

Slowly I developed my ideas about the dreaming body, and the students loved it. But my older colleagues were not happy. I had, of course, core friends, but those few others were not happy with me, and I could not understand why. But now I am thankful to them, because then I realized, "Oh, maybe I should do my own thing now?" And processwork began.

Had I been aware of my childhood dream, things would have been smoother. My father symbol in the childhood dream would have said, "When clients come and ask you to do something you are not trained for, try your best." And the bear would have said, "Let's move out and develop new things!"

Today, I am back in wonderful contact with the Jungians just about everywhere. Remember, who you are is a gift, and if you know your gift, it will reduce the tensions around you. If you have ongoing inner problems or conflict with someone these are due, in part, to your not knowing enough about your own childhood dream pattern. Life went fine the way it did. Today the Jungian community is very open to dreambody work.

My basic point is that *our biggest global problem is that we leave global change to fate or to world leaders.* We think *they* should be doing better. Instead, each of us, each in our own way, needs to follow our 1st dream patterns and dreaming process. Maybe your way is to meditate. Maybe your way is to paint. Maybe your way is to dance. Maybe your way is to speak out in the world. Each has their own way—there is no one way. If everyone follows their own way, world change for all will happen more smoothly.

Therefore, I am voting for you to make world change with your great spirit. If you want to work with leaders or others in your organization, and wonder how to do this with people who are not ready for inner work, first take their side, and say to them, "You have probably not heard much about inner work in business? This is business! Let's make money. Let's resolve organizational problems!" Then, you might say, "Here is a quick method. So let's relax and be quick, and use only 5 minutes for inner work. We can talk about it afterwards." I guarantee even the largest world organizations will agree to that today. It can be exciting and relaxing. Appreciate the primary process of the organization and bring in 5 minutes of inner work to begin with. Next time, they might ask you to do it for 6 minutes.

OK! Let's do a 5 minute 2nd Training exercise on world issues.

Exercise: Use Your World Leadership Process to Center Yourself and Help All

(Triad—one person works, one is the reader, one will play the X. Switch 3 times. Or, just do this by yourself.)

1. Imagine and note down a group or national or international problem that upsets you most. Act out with gestures and words the roles you favor and the X role and energy you don't like in that situation. *(If another person is present, take note of this X role energy so you can play it later).* Make notes.

2. Recall 2 or 3 of your 1st dream/memory figures and energies. Note, FEEL, and act out their energies. Then, imagine and describe to yourself (or triad partners) how you might use these powers to work with that world problem in some useful way. Make notes.

3. Now, explore your *phase 4 unpredictable processmind experience.* That is, stand if possible, and carefully, be moved spontaneously. Wait for repetitive motions. Do you sense how your basic childhood dream pattern/ energies appear in some of those movements and gestures? How do your spontaneous movements and experiences add or suggest tips to help with that world problem? Tell your triad partners about this and make notes.

4. *(Read this whole paragraph first, before doing it)* Now, you or a third person, act out that world problem and its troublesome X role and energy. You—work with that world problem by bringing in your dream pattern energies and universe experience where you feel they are needed to help the situation. Third person, please notice

if and when you are changed, or where a cool spot, or relaxation happens. Stop there and give feedback to the person working. Third person playing X: Notice when something changes you, even if it is very slight. Don't press yourself to just keep going on. Remember, a cool spot insight can make a big difference, discovering what relaxed the world problem.

5. Person working on the world problem, make notes about your learning. Re-formulate your first dream as your *Leadership Pattern* to help and change the world. Write this down! Finally, plan to *show and tell your friends and our world* about how you use your first dream energies and universe experience to help the world.

One seminar participant told me, "This wonderful experience led me to a mu-shin experience." That reminded me of Suzuki's explanation of the mu-shin term: "Being free from mind-attachment."[38] In the 2nd Training, mu-shin is a #4 fluid experience, a phase we go through.

The 2nd Training simply reminds you that you are gifted with dreaming, fluidity, spontaneity, and leadership. Your leadership is part of your spontaneous processmind experience. It follows your greatest gift: your childhood dream pattern and the spirit that moves you.

Remember, you are gifted. You were born with a dream-gift. We all need *your way* of doing things to help our world. Believe in your basic nature. Use it with the open and creative mind of your 2nd Training, and our world will change for the better.

CONCLUSION

Leave Earth in 100 Years for Survival? . . . No!

. . .

OUR PERSONAL LIVES, RELATIONSHIPS, FAMILIES, organizations, cultures, and countries need eldership. Because of our planet's social, political, and ecological problems, the world we share is asking you and me for our 2nd Training leadership support.

Stephen Hawking and other well-known physicists said we will need to leave our earth in 100 years' time, because it will become uninhabitable for human life. Most people want to ignore this, but I suggest that we learn to work together to avoid this global crisis.

We can create a more sustainable world if more of us learn to process tensions in our own life, relationships, businesses, communities, and world. My point has been to realize and actualize your 2nd Training. Otherwise, we will continue wars and lack the kind of relationships needed to work together for a more livable planet. Therefore, all of us should work with troublesome conflicts with more awareness.

Just before writing this conclusion, I wondered if I would be able to model the 2nd Training and work on severe conflicts, because I have not had a big conflict with anyone for more than 20 years. Then suddenly, I got into a conflict! That was a big "Woof!"

Amy and I were trying to park, and another person in another car nearby screamed, "That's my spot!" Actually, that was a general parking spot, so I got confused and said, "I thought that spot belonged to the city. No?"

And this person yelled, "NO!"

I realized I was in trouble. Then I remembered I was going to write about the worst conflict you have ever had, and now, suddenly, one such conflict was beginning!

So, I said, defensively but politely, "I think I was here first. I am going to park here."

The other person screamed, *"NO! This is my SPOT!"*

I said, "Well, I did not realize your name was on here. I thought it belonged to the city."

He said, "That is my spot! You better move or else!"

At first, all the bad words you can imagine in English, French, German, Greek, Italian, Spanish, Russian, Japanese and so forth started coming out of both of our mouths. I realized I needed the 2nd Training I am suggesting in this book.

I remembered the coming exercise I had been studying and asked myself, "How am I like that person I am in an intense conflict with?" What a question!

The question I asked myself is a self-reflective question. That is, *"How I am like the other?"*

I am not like that usually, and I did not like the question; but I had to admit—yes, I am like that, a little bit.

How? I remember about 20 years ago, one of my relatives and I did not agree about certain things. I got angry and was a bit like that guy on the street, yelling about the parking spot. "Grrr!" I said to my relative, "I am not going to talk with you again!" because I was so upset. Actually, we did talk again.

But in any case, I am a little bit like the person I was against. Not exactly, but a little bit. Knowing that I (and you) can be like the monsters we are fighting can enable us to communicate better, even in extreme circumstances. Such communication can make life on our planet more sustainable. It is the core of phase 3 in the 2nd Training.

In the parking situation, everything quieted down when I said to him, "I understand. I am like you, sometimes." The problem was not solved, but for the moment, things quieted down.

My big point is this: *If you are fighting somebody and the other one is the only bad one—that is normal. You may need to fight, but you can do better.* If we all continue without a 2nd Training, we will hasten war, climate change, and the end of human life on this planet.

As I have said before, in the 2nd Training, you need to take a hard stand in #2. *But remember phase 3, where you realize you are somehow like the other.* Knowing this cools the conflict, reduces violence, and creates a better world. It certainly relaxed me and cooled off the situation.

Remember, we hurt our environment by getting overheated and thereby overheating our environment. We need to leave our ordinary state of mind, remember the 2nd Training, and flow better with events. This includes, especially, phase 3. This will cool things off, at least temporarily, so we can work on things better together.

WORLD SOLUTIONS

Let's wake up and integrate the universe to help our fears about the earth's future. Let's be more conscious of how we do things now, here on earth. In other words, we don't need to die as a human race, but we do need to *die* out of consensus reality more often to connect to the 2nd Training, the dreaming universe, to process our conflicts. Let's learn to create community.

Connecting to the Great Spirit in phase 4 may enable miracles to happen! All of us will eventually age and leave the physical form. So, whenever we think about aging, we should also let ourselves *be moved* by the universe. That is the #4 experience. Then, use your awareness and notice how you and all conflicts around you flow better and go through phases.

The core of the 2nd Training. Let yourself go, in dreaming, every time you think about problems. Learn to fight, and switch roles, and let go, at least temporarily. Dying—in the sense of letting go—should be part of life. Let's not wait till you are 40, 60, 80, or 120 to let go. Don't use your own deteriorating physiology or our earth's demise to force you into the 2nd Training.

Physicist John Wheeler gave Albert Einstein a special gift on his 75th birthday.[39]

Wheeler said that the universe self-reflects. That is, the math of physics makes the universe appear to look at itself. He suggested to Einstein that the universe tends to reflect on itself, a reflection found in the math of quantum physics.

REMEMBER SELF-REFLECTION

You are whatever fascinates you, whatever you love or hate. In other words, I was that nasty person at the parking space. You, too, are whatever you don't like to look at. It reflects you.

40. Self-Reflection

Your more primary process says, "Oh, no! Not me! I don't look like that disgusting creature! I will never look like that!" But yes—in some way, and at some point, you have looked like that.

Then, recall phase 3 and *learn to self-reflect in the* 2nd Training. This is a very simple psychological thing, in principle! If you think about a group or person that you don't like, resist them, but explain how you are like them, as well.

One of our biggest earth and psychological problems is that we repress reflection and dreaming. We repress and ignore our earth, our ageing and grey hair, and we make enemies out of everything and everyone we don't like. Some follow their beloved spiritual beliefs, but most forget to self-reflect!

Because the universe is self-reflective, everything that catches your attention is about you. We need to see that *everything we see on the outside is us.*

Take our love for the sky and our 13.8 billion-year-old universe. That is ancient, and we are only very young in comparison. But we, too, are this ancient universe!

THE UNIVERSE AND THE 2ND TRAINING

When you let go and let the universe move you, gravity, your psychology, and the universe's mysterious essence (its dark energy and dark matter, which are 95% of the universe), move you in a detached, essence level of experience that can elder our world. I talk more about dark energy and dark matter in the Appendix; but let me just mention that only 5% of the universe's energy and matter is known. We are, in part, being pulled, pushed, and moved by very mysterious forces in our universe.

41. The Universe (Thanks to BBC)

As we have seen in previous chapters, *if you really let go in phase 4, your childhood dream pattern will pattern your behavior.* When you let go and dance, you will become what you were originally, and you will be able to help our world more.

Then, as you activate your 2nd Training, big problems will get easier as you realize that at least in a small way, you are like your opponents. Don't wait till the end of life or when you feel threatened by the end of the world. Integrate those fears now.

Your 2nd Training integrates the fear of earth-demise experiences now. Then, even things you dislike in consensus reality—things you need to fight—will be easier to work with.

Remember to use your awareness. Don't make a rule out of detachment. In the 2nd Training, there is an openness to fighting in phase 2. Try to relax in phase 1, forget troubles, and in phase 2, protect yourself, and try to stop the other.

But in phase 3, be self-reflective. Realize you are both yourself and the other. If you feel that way, you will be able to relate to just about anyone: people who love or hate you. The following exercise might help.

EXERCISE: 2ND TRAINING FOR PEACE IN CONFLICT (in dyads)

1. What person (X) bothers you most?
2. Imagine #2 fighting with X in consensus reality.
3. Sense #4 and relax. And in #3, reflect—switch roles and be X. How are you, or how have you been, X? And how would you like them to change? Can you make that change?
4. Explain to X (now played by a partner) how you are X and how you plan to make the changes you require from X.
5. Relax in #4 and drop all problems. (Or go through phases again, to relax conflict)

Demonstration with Arny.

Amy: What X person bothers you most, Arny?

Arny: That guy in the parking area. I thought that problem would turn into a fist fight.

Amy: Can you imagine phase 2: fighting him, in consensus reality?

Arny: I can imagine. I am glad I did not have to. But if I did, I would have said, "You are an idiot!!"

Amy: Sense phase 4.

Arny: OK. [feels into the phase 4 movement].

Amy: When you have a sense of #4, explore #3. That is, switch roles and be the X.

Arny: [Plays the man in the parking area] That parking spot is *my* spot! I will fight you! Get the hell out of *my* spot!

Amy: As you do that, maybe you get the sense of how you are that X person, with that behavior.

Arny: I worked on that, and what I found, as I said before, is that I, too, have had that Grrrr energy. And I recalled the relative I had a conflict with, many years ago.

Amy: How would you like that X guy in the parking lot to change?

Arny: He should cool off.

Amy: Now, explain to the X, played by your partner, how you are the X. And how you plan to make the changes you require of him.

Arny: Amy, can you act him out?

Amy: (As X) Get out of my space! I am threatening you! Get out of there, right now!

Arny: My first reaction is #2—and my fist comes up!

Amy: (Playing X, escalating conflict) Get out of there! Didn't you see that parking spot is mine? What's wrong with you?

Arny: What is wrong with me? I lose my temper. I know what that is like! I am totally with you, dear X. I understand your angry feelings. I, too, am like that.

Amy: (As X) I did not expect this . . .

Arny: We don't have to be friends, but I want to thank you for waking me up to myself!

Amy: Oh. How will you make the changes you require of X in yourself?

Arny: I won't turn against this person. I will try to remain open, though careful.

Amy: (As X) How would you be open to me, in the moment? Before, your wanting to remain open and saying you are like me confused me: that cooled me off.

Arny: I understand where you are coming from, insisting that the parking spot is yours.

Amy: (As X) THIS SPOT IS MINE! Can't you see that?

Arny: Perhaps it really is yours. If I had not already parked there, I would give it to you, but I have to go, now. Sorry. I hope I am able to give you something more in the future.

Amy: You partially agreeing with me relaxed me.

Arny: Thanks. If and when I see him on the street, I will remember generosity.

The 2nd Training process is a fluid awareness process, moving with and through phases:

1. *Repress*

2. *Struggle with X*

3. *Realize how you are X*

4. *Follow the universe.*

Feedback, after the class does the exercise.

P: I worked on Trump. What I hate most about him is—he is so narcissistic and full of himself. He knows everything. So, I had to really work to recognize that in myself. I then noticed that *my hatred of him is very similar to his "Trumpiness."* I am 100% sure I am much better than him—which is just like him! Wow!

Arny: Great work!

R: I worked with this bossy person, this man I have worked on for decades—I was trying to facilitate a group process and he took it over, before I even opened my mouth. He basically said, "We don't want you!" I have worked on it in many ways, but not like this. I became him and then I had to change, and I had to *let go of control and trust the process* and not be bossy.

Arny: How are you a little bit like him?

R: I tend to want to control the process. I want to tell people what to do. I want to do it my way. That is not even that hard to say—I recognize it in myself! That's 2nd Training inner work—it means, for me, loving all of myself!

J: I worked with corporations because part of my work is figuring out how to deal with their system problems.

Arny: How are you like corporations?

J: Well, corporations must make money for their stockholders. Fossil fuel corporations put carbon into the air and create global warming! Then, in phase 3, I realized I have to let go of my own desire for a corporate death penalty; otherwise I am like them—putting murderous stuff in the air. I wanted a corporate death penalty—but if I am really honoring what I am expecting of them, I cannot hold onto my anger. I have to reconcile, restore, redirect, and find ways of negotiating. . . . Then, I can be in a long-term relationship with these folks!

Arny: I am going to clap, for that! All of this reminds me of an incredible wisdom associated with the Native American Cherokee traditions. They said:

> *"Never judge a person unless you have walked*
> *a mile in their moccasins."*

42. Walk a mile . . .

I could not trace exactly where this quote came from on the internet, and I still want to honor the Cherokee, and all our Native American ancestors.

If you are in tension or conflict, remember phase 3: don't judge the other *until you have walked a mile in their shoe*s. It will make the 2nd Training a little easier.

Remember the 2nd Training, and remain open to all phases, that is, don't make a rule out of any of its phases:

Phase 1: Have a good day! Take it easy. Relax.

Phase 2: Speak out. Protect! Take your side!

Phase 3: Switch roles, *and walk in the other's shoes. . . .*

Phase 4: Listen and be moved by the sound of silence. Let *it* resolve problems.

Don't make it a program to be hostile, or nice. Rather, follow the changing process, that is, the spirit of the 2nd Training, in order to flow with conflict and peace, inside and outside, for a better world.

APPENDIX

A Big TOE

• • •

VARIOUS PHYSICISTS SUCH AS STEPHEN Hawking have predicted that within 100 years, the Earth will not be able to support human life.[40] That means that babies born today may not be able to live on this planet. Too few people today want to think about this problem.

Hawking's statement is a challenging wakeup call; yet most people are in phase 1: they don't want to be bothered about the future of the planet. However, if we go on like this, our planet will continue to degenerate and create severe human health issues. Already our air in many places on earth is becoming unhealthy to breathe, the planet's temperature is continuously rising, the icecaps continue melting, and flooding of lowlands occurs. These are serious problems.

43. Stephen Hawking
(Thanks Wikipedia)

Constant battles and wars increase global heating. Just think of the dying people, burning buildings and bombs. If all this continues, human life on this planet will become impossible, possibly within 100 years—as Hawking and other physicists have suggested. Everyone needs to study what we can do to save our planet.

The previous chapters about the 2nd Training give us hope about reducing conflicts, and I personally believe, at this point at least, that we can change things on earth for the better. I am not quite as negative as Stephen Hawking or other physicists.

An amazing event happened as I began to give a Portland class, from which this appendix was derived. Just before the class, the news appeared on my computer that Stephen Hawking had died!

Amy adds, "Yes. After finishing, you started talking about Stephen Hawking. You could not stop—you were so driven. Every sentence was about him. Then, suddenly, the news came on, announcing that he had just died. It was amazing. I never saw you like that."

I loved Hawking because of his physics and because of his strength to continue, despite severe health issues. I loved his great mind and the way he thought about the universe. He warned that if the world goes on the way it is now going, it is doomed in 100 years' time, for human life. It seems to me and others at this point at least, that if we must leave the earth, our next stop might be Mars. But living on Mars will be more than complicated!

However, the 2nd Training can reduce our earth-based problems, conflicts, and global warming. The reason I am not quite as negative about the future is because I am sure the 2nd Training can help us work together for a better One World.

ONE WORLD

Hawking was thinking about physics and was less in contact with psychology and worldwork. Amy and I travel around the world a lot and see, feel, and hear how our planet is involved in one large group process. Our planet, composed of different nations, different racial and ethnic groups, with different planetary problems, will soon be forced to focus on one problem—human survival.

The world's future needs us to work together, and we need to bring our sciences, psychologies, and our religions together. Right now, they are as split as some warring nations!

Part of the missing unifying feeling can arise with the 2nd Training's reflection in phase 3. Recall quantum theory and that John Wheeler and others suggested that our universe self-reflects![41] As I have said, we all need to reflect on what we see as parts of us. As the concluding chapter showed, *we need to walk in the other's shoes to relieve problems.*

Part of our world's potential unification depends upon each of us getting in touch and living with the essence level, the gods, and Tao that moves us. To do that, we need to see how our belief systems and sciences fit together. Please see the diagrams that follow. They suggest how Taoism, Processwork, Physics, and Religions might be related. Note the essence level in Physics has a note about Dark Matter and Dark Energy. I write about dark matter and dark energy in the next pages.

44. Big TOE (Big Theory Of Everything)				
Methods / *Levels*	Taoism	Process-work	Physics	Religion
Essence	Tao that can't be said	Essence #4 altered state	Dark energy, dark matter, quantum waves	God experiences, invisible powers
Reflection (level just prior to dreams)	Coins catch and reflect the Tao	Notice and reflect "flirts" (flickering in our attention)	Reflection in quantum theory's math	Meditate + reflect, God tips; e.g. "turn other cheek"
Dreamland	Coins give rise to Yin-Yang + trigram images	Flirts appear in dreams and fantasies	Elementary particles + atoms	God images and dream-like experiences
Consensus Reality	Hexagrams describing real events	CR events + everyday life	Easily measurable objects	Suggested beliefs, rules of behavior

45. Processwork's Phases   **Taoism's Trigram Process**

Processwork's 2nd Training
MEANS SENSING #4, and
FLOWING WITH ALL PHASES;
that is:
Follow and Flow with the TAO, as it changes.

This Big TOE and its diagram is an early first attempt to formulate a Big Theory of Everything, or Big TOE. This is meant to stimulate our unification thinking for the future. The Big TOE implies how processwork ideas are linked to spiritual, psychological, and physical theories, and brings these various methods and belief systems closer together.

Many people will reject this attempt. For example, some of my physicist friends often reject religion. "What are you doing with God concepts? You can't measure them!"

I would answer, "I want to connect physics and religion, Taoism, and processwork because they are all different aspects describing our total reality. Physics speaks mostly about measurable reality but don't forget—some of its basic concepts, such as dark matter and quantum waves, are not yet understood. Yet we need these ideas to understand other measurable aspects of reality. And remember, the real and imaginary numbers in physics and real and imaginary aspects of our universe correspond with just about all human experiences."

THINK ABOUT WAR

Today, our present psychology, Taoism, religion, and physics *do not deal well enough* with war or climate change. Present knowledge is NOT enough to create needed world change. However, if we begin to put the sciences and belief systems together in a Big TOE, perhaps we can deal with world issues better, as I have indicated in this book.

THE ESSENCE LEVEL

See my suggested Big TOE chart. Taoism's essence level is called *the Tao that can't be said*. In other words, we experience something but cannot formulate it in words. We read from Laozi (Lao Tzu), in *Tao Te Ching* Ch. 1,[42] (as translated by Gia-Fu Feng & Jane English, 1974):

> *The Tao that can be told is not the eternal Tao;*
> *The name that can be named is not the eternal name.*
> The nameless is the beginning of heaven and earth.
> The named is the mother of ten thousand things.
> Ever desireless, one can see the mystery.
> Ever desiring, one can see the manifestations.
> These two spring from the same source but differ in name;
> This appears as darkness.
> Darkness within darkness.
> The gate to all mystery.

We read here that "The nameless is the beginning of heaven and earth." *That nameless mystery, that darkness, is what we have been calling the essence level.* The Tao is the background power or force that flips the coin into a dreamland image. Dreamland, in Taoism, is the result of the Tao moving a coin this way or that way, creating the beginning of images and trigrams.

In processwork, I call the "Tao that can't be said" the processmind intelligence at the essence level, an intelligence that moves the coin about in a meaningful manner to create yin-yang trigram images. The force moving the coin is like what today's physics calls "dark matter" or processwork's essence level. The resulting trigram coming from coin flips is a dream-like experience, not quite real yet, in terms of consensus, measurable, understandable reality.

Essence in Psychology and Taoism

While some therapists think about the meaning of dreams, I feel that not only is the dream and its meaning important, but also the essence power that creates the images. I think of that power as the Tao that can't be said, as the essence level. So, the essence level has a tendency to self-reflect (like the equations of quantum theory). This creates dreamlike figures which, with associations, become realizable ideas in consensus reality.

What is the essence level in physics? Quantum waves are a bit like the essence level. The waves are both empirical and theoretical. What those quantum waves are, no one knows for certain. You will remember that those quantum waves, when looked at, transform from wave-like forms into particles. Quantum waves in physics are like the essence level in processwork.

DARK MATTER

Notice that I put dark energy on the chart at the essence level in physics—but I have not yet discussed it. Dark energy (and dark matter) are not yet understood in physics. Dark energy and matter are essence-like. Nobody yet knows exactly what they are. Dark energy and matter are measurable but up to now, incomprehensible. We notice their effects in the universe, but don't understand dark matter or dark energy.

We realize, however, that 95% of the universe is dark energy and matter. What we see and understand about the universe is only 5% of it. Yes—only 5%! The other 95% of the universe is unknown. (Dark matter is about 25%, and dark energy, about 70%.)

How do we know dark energy and matter are there? Because galaxies hold together more than we can predict from the known matter. So we speak of that extra gravitational effect as dark matter. We notice the effect, but otherwise know nothing about dark matter—except that it creates that gravitational effect.

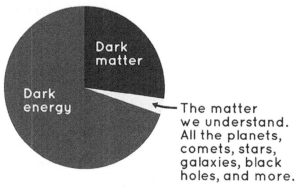

46. Dark matter & dark energy (Thanks NASA)

We know that dark energy exists, as well. Why? Because some unknown energy is bending light waves in the universe more than we can understand. No one knows (yet) where that (bending) energy comes from. So, physics calls that bending ability "dark energy". It is 70% of our universe.

To sum up dark matter and energy, see the diagram from NASA.[43]

The diagram shows that the matter and energy we understand, including the planets, comets, stars, galaxies, black holes and so forth, comprise only 5% of the universe. The other 95% of the universe, physics calls dark energy and dark matter. Dark matter and energy are weird, but the essence level of psychology is also weird!

Most of who you are is unknown! In a way, the Tao that can't be said or *essence level may well also be 95% of our psychology.* Perhaps it is the energy of deep, indescribable feelings, the energy behind dreaming and perhaps life itself—which up to now, no one quite understands. We can measure your weight, but not the spirit that animates you. We are never completely certain what psychological heaviness or lightness is about. We don't really understand where your dreaming excitement comes from, or what life is.

But we do know that "dark" essence level feeling is the core of the 2nd Training. Yes, dark energy and matter are aspects of the essence level. Perhaps we are moved, like the universe, by energies and gravitational forces that cannot be measured yet.

However, if you relax, breathe, and let yourself be moved, you notice new dreams and ideas coming up. In psychology, we could say the processmind can be felt, but its origins are mysterious and perhaps

47. Orchid (Thanks Wikipedia)

connected to the universe. Perhaps the essence level is 95% of our psychology, and like dark energy and matter in the universe, the essence level can be experienced, but is basically a noncognitive experience or field power intelligence.

The essence level and the processmind in psychology, and dark energy in physics, move us unpredictably but meaningfully. Let me use this orchid to explain our dark energy or processmind energy. Here is a flower (a long-stemmed orchid). See or imagine the flower moving. Now, imagine there is no wind, and it still moves. Dark matter and dark energy are like the "no wind" that moves things. You cannot understand that "dark wind," yet it moves you as if you were a flower blowing in a wind that cannot be measured.

When something moves us, but we don't know what it is, it is like the Tao that can't be said. Dark energy and dark matter bring us close to religious ideas. Too close, for some physicists! Are the gods moving the flowers? ☺

Perhaps like dark matter and energy, what I have been calling "the essence level" is 95% of reality. My point for psychology, physics, and religion is that we need to be open to something we can feel but cannot yet completely comprehend. The mysterious essence level and the powers of the essence level connect Taoism, psychology, physics, and religions.

RELIGION

If religion did not exist, it would have to! When I was skiing in the mountains, I noticed people looking at the great white snow-capped mountain and saying, "Oh, wow! God! That's beautiful!" Now, why are they talking about God like that?

The word "God" is used in these situations as an expression of amazement at some unknown natural power or beauty that cannot be exactly formulated . . . at least in words, in the beginning. In other words, the essence level is an invisible power that is felt and imagined by some, in connection with a dreamland image of a particular God.

UNIVERSAL RELIGION?

Depending upon the community and the location around the world, when we notice something awesome, we create names for that awesome natural and almost invisible power. However, in spite of the many names, perhaps there is one universal religion that might be called "Love for Nature."

Different communities create their own views and religions and often feel that their beliefs are different from other religions, because their dreamland images and their consensus reality formulations differ.

I appreciate those differences. Yet there seems to be a universal nature experience in the background, an essence level. Perhaps that experience is also connected with dark energy and dark matter. In any case, in dreamland, specific figures and the messages of God appear, depending upon the community. I love the diversity of many different community experiences and explanations of this great nature power.

Frequently, we repress the feeling of what moves us—not only in religion, but also in psychology and in physics. When dark matter, dreams, and the Great Spirit move us, we mostly repress that essence experience, and stay instead with dreamland images and consensus reality descriptions. "Thou shalt do this, and thou shalt not do that."

For many people, depending upon who you are and which group you associate yourself with, rules can be very meaningful. But neglecting the essence we all share stresses the differences between groups—which leads to community diversity and, also, to community conflict.

Yet, go anywhere—to the forest, watch sunset in the city, go to the coast and watch the beach—let yourself be moved by an unknown dark energy-power, and in principle, you may sense or rediscover the gods.

To address religious disagreements, start with the awesome experience we all share: "Oh, my God!" Go to the common ground. Go to the essence level—an experience we all share of the powers of the universe. It is a "wow!" experience. Perhaps, as in physics, that essence experience is 95% of what moves us.

Start with what we share and then stress the differences as very important, so other people do not have to. In a way, we are all closer to one another and all part of one spiritual family. Don't forget the connection of the essence level with dark matter and dark energy, the unknown powers moving and bending things. Recall "Oh, God!"—especially if you don't know what is next in your life, or how to manage conflict with the 2nd Training.

If you stay a little closer to that essence level, remembering that it might be 95% of reality, you will be more fluid and aware of changing phases, especially during times of conflict. Then, the 2nd Training and life itself can be easier and more amazing—at least sometimes . . . even during impossible times.

Bibliography

Accelerating Expansion of the Universe. 2018, 20 Aug. Retrieved from https://en.wikipedia.org/wiki/Accelerating_expansion_of_the_universe

Boyer, Carl B., & Merzbach, Uta C. 2011. *A History of Mathematics* (3rd ed.). New York, NY: Wiley.

Brewster, Fanny. 2017. *African Americans and Jungian Psychology: Leaving the Shadows*. New York, NY: Routledge.

Chief Seattle. n.d. There is no death. Retrieved from https://www.brainyquote.com/search_results?q=There+is+no+death

Copying Beethoven. 2006. Quotes. Retrieved from https://www.imdb.com/title/tt0424908/quotes

Copying Beethoven. 2018. Quote. Retrieved from https://en.wikipedia.org/wiki/Copying_Beethoven

Dovey, Dana. 2017, 26 Dec. Stephen Hawking's Six Wildest Predictions From 2017—From a Robot Apocalypse to the Demise of Earth. *Newsweek*. Retrieved from https://www.newsweek.com/stephen-hawking-end-year-predictions-2017-755952

Feynman, Richard. 2010. *The Feynman Lectures on Physics*. Pasadena, CA: California Institute of Technology Press.

Glatz, Carol. 2016, 29 Nov. Pope Francis meets Stephen Hawking at Vatican science conference. *Catholic Herald.* Retrieved from http://www.catholicherald.co.uk/news/2016/11/29/pope-francis-meets-stephen-hawking-at-vatican-science-confe rence/

Hawking, Stephen. 2017, June 9. "Humanity has 100 years left on Earth." YouTube video. Retrieved from https://www. youtube.com/watch?v=RAYQL4raMZc

Jung, C.G. 1950. *Psychologische Interpretation von Kinderträumen und älterer Literatur über Kinderträume. 2 Bände. Seminar von Prof. Dr. C.G. Jung Wintersemester 1938/39.* Zurich, Switzerland: Verlag. Retrieved from https://zentralbuchhandlung.de/itm/ psychologische-interpretation-von-kindertraeumen-und-aelterer-literatur-ueber-kindertraeume-2-baende-4237.html

Lake, James. 2018. The near-death experience. *Psychology Today.* Retrieved from https://www.psychologytoday.com/us/blog/ integrative-mental-health-care/201705/the-near-death-experience-nde

Lao Tsu. 1934. *The Way and Its Power: A Study of the Tao Te Ching* (Arthur Waley, Trans.). Reprinted 2011 by Literary Licensing, LLC.

Lao Tsu. 1974. *Tao Te Ching* (Gia-Fu Feng & Jane English, Trans.). New York, NY: Vintage.

Laozi. 2018, 17 Aug. *Tao Te Ching.* Retrieved from https://en. wikiquote.org/wiki/Laozi

Mindell, Amy, & Mindell, Arnold. 1992. *Riding the Horse Backwards.* Penguin / Arkana. Republished by Lao Tse Press (Portland, OR), 2002; by Deep Democracy Exchange (Portland OR / CreateSpace IPP), 2016.

Mindell, Arnold. 2017. *Conflict: Phases, Forums, and Solutions.* North Charleston, SC: CreateSpace IPP/ World Tao Press.

———. 2013. *Dance of the Ancient One.* Portland, OR: Deep Democracy Exchange.

———. 2010. *ProcessMind: A User's Guide to Connecting with the Mind of God.* Wheaton, IL: Quest Books.

———. 2007. *Earth-Based Psychology: Path Awareness from the Teachings of Don Juan, Richard Feynman, and Lao Tse.* Portland, OR: Lao Tse Press.

———. 2004. *The Quantum Mind and Healing: How to Listen and Respond to Your Body's Symptoms.* Charlottesville, VA: Hampton Roads.

———. 2002. *The Deep Democracy of Open Forums: How to Transform Organizations into Communities.* Charlottesville, VA: Hampton Roads.

———. 2001. *The Dreammaker's Apprentice.* Charlottesville, VA: Hampton Roads.

———. 2000. *Dreaming While Awake: Techniques for 24-Hour Lucid Dreaming.* Charlottesville, VA: Hampton Roads.

———. 2000. *The Quantum Mind: The Edge Between Physics and Psychology.* Portland, OR: Lao Tse Press. Reprinted by Deep Democracy Exchange (Portland, OR), 2014.

———. 1995. *Sitting in the Fire: Large Group Transformation Through Diversity and Conflict.* Portland, OR: Lao Tse Press. Reprinted by Deep Democracy Exchange (Portland, OR), 2014.

———. 1993. *The Shaman's Body: A New Shamanism for Health, Relationships and Community.* San Francisco, CA: Harper Collins.

————. 1992. *The Leader as Martial Artist: An Introduction to Deep Democracy.* San Francisco, CA: Harper Collins. Reprinted by Deep Democracy Exchange (Portland, OR), 2000.

————. 1991. *Working on Yourself Alone.* Portland, OR: Lao Tse Press. Reprinted by Deep Democracy Exchange (Portland, OR), 2000.

————. 1989. *Coma, Key to Awakening: Working with the Dreambody Near Death.* Boston, MA: Shambhala. Reprinted as *Coma: The Dreambody Near Death,* by Lao Tse Press (Portland, OR), 2009.

————. 1989. *The Year One: Global Process Work.* London & New York: Viking-Penguin-Arkana. Reprinted by Deep Democracy Exchange (Portland, OR) in 2002.

————. 1988. *City Shadows.* London & New York: Routledge. Reprinted by Deep Democracy Exchange (Portland, OR), 2008.

————. 1987. *The Dreambody in Relationships.* London & New York: Viking-Penguin-Arkana. Reprinted by Lao Tse Press (Portland, OR), 2000; Deep Democracy Exchange (Portland, OR), 2002.

————. 1985. *River's Way.* Portland, OR: Lao Tse Press. Reprinted by Deep Democracy Exchange (Portland, OR), 2002.

————. 1985. *Working with the Dreaming Body.* London, UK: Routledge & Kegan Paul. Reprinted by Viking-Penguin-Arkana (London & New York), 1989; Lao Tse Press (Portland, OR), 2002; CreateSpace IPP/ Deep Democracy Exchange (Portland, OR), 2014.

————. 1982. *Dreambody: The Body's Role in Revealing the Self.* Boston, MASAD Sigo Press. Reprinted by Viking-

Penguin-Arkana (London & New York), 1986; by Lao Tse Press (Portland, OR), 2000; by Deep Democracy Exchange (Portland, OR), 2011.

NASA. 2017, 22 March. Dark Matter. Retrieved from https://spaceplace.nasa.gov/dark-matter/en/

Rumi. n.d. Quotes. Retrieved from http://www.greatthoughts treasury.com/author/rumi-fully-jal%C4%81l-ad-d%C4% ABn-mu%E1%B8%A5ammad-rumi

Suzuki, Daisetz Teitaro. 1994. *Manual of Zen Buddhism.* New York, NY: Grove Press

Tao. 2017, 13 Sept. Quote. Retrieved from https://en.wikiquote.org/wiki/Tao

Theory of Everything. 2018, 25 August. Retrieved from https://en.wikipedia.org/wiki/Theory_of_everything

Thomas, Bill. 2011, 3 Feb. Gerotranscendance. Retrieved from https://changingaging.org/aging101/gerotranscendence/

To the Great Spirit. 2017. Retrieved from http://www.marquette.edu/faith/prayers-lakota.php

Verse of Light. 2018, 29 May. Retrieved from https://en.wikipedia.org/wiki/Verse_of_light

Worldwork. 2017. Deep Democracy in a World of Divides. Retrieved from http://worldwork.org/worldwork-2017-greece/theme/

Index

. . .

End Notes

. . .

1. https://en.wikipedia.org/wiki/Theory_of_everything

2. Humanity has 100 years left on Earth: Stephen Hawking - YouTube https://www.youtube.com/watch?v=RAYQL4raMZc

3. https://en.wikipedia.org/wiki/Theory_of_everything

4. for more about processwork, see www.aamindell.net

5. http://catholicherald.co.uk/news/2016/11/29/pope-francis-meets-stephen-hawking-at-vatican-science-conference/

6. Big TOE ideas can be found in the Appendix of this book

7. Feynman, Richard; *The Feynman Lectures on Physics,* 2010, California Institute of Technology.

8. *Quantum Mind;* https://www.amazon.com/Quantum-Mind-Between-Physics-Psychology/dp/1619710129/ref=pd_lpo_sbs_14_t_2?_encoding=UTF8&psc=1&refRID=KWAW0HZQE1R1X654VFCP

9. See my book, *Coma, Key to Awakening.*

10. *A History of Mathematics,* Carl B. Boyer & Uta C. Merzbach.

11. *Conflict: Phases, Forums, and Solutions*

12. The Jungian analyst, Fanny Brewster, writing in *African Americans and Jungian Psychology: Leaving the Shadows.* New York, NY: Routledge, 2017.

13. https://www.psychologytoday.com/us/blog/integrative-mental-health-care/201705/the-near-death-experience-nde

14. https://www.pinterest.com.au/pin/5299470811317222797/?lp=true

15. Thanks to https://commons.wikimedia.org/wiki/File:Albert_Einstein_Head.jpg

16. See for example, my books, *Coma, Key to Awakening,* and *City Shadows.*

17. Thanks Wikipedia and Amy Mindell for finding this picture

18. See my book, the *Shaman's Body.* https://www.amazon.com/Shamans-Body-Shamanism-Transforming-Relationships/dp/0062506552/ref=sr_1_1?ie=UTF8&qid=1529464563&sr=8-1&keywords=shaman%27s+body

19. https://www.jpl.nasa.gov/spaceimages/details.php?id=PIA16881

20. https://www.imdb.com/title/tt0424908/quotes

21. https://en.wikipedia.org/wiki/Copying_Beethoven

22. https://en.wikipedia.org/wiki/Verse_of_light

23. http://www.marquette.edu/faith/prayers-lakota.php

24. https://www.google.com/search?q=Game+of+Thrones,+zombie&client=firefox-b-1-ab&tbm=isch&tbo=u&source=univ&sa=X&ved=0ahUKEwiXj6DW28fbAhWsIDQIHeSWDQYQsAQIfA&biw=1133&bih=503#imgrc=w8abTXMC-_7RdM:

25. http://worldwork.org/worldwork-2017-greece/theme/

26. https://www.linkedin.com/in/h-grady-gray-ph-d-23042569/

27. https://www.brainyquote.com/search_results?q=There+is+no+death

28. An ashram (especially in South Asia) a hermitage, monastic community, or other place of religious retreat.

29. http://www.greatthoughtstreasury.com/author/rumi-fully-jal%C4%81l-ad-d%C4%ABn-mu%E1%B8%A5ammad-rumi

30. *Dreambody, The Body's Role in Revealing the Self.*

31. https://en.wikipedia.org/wiki/Nicolaus_Copernicus

32. https://en.wikipedia.org/wiki/Johannes_Kepler

33. See Wikipedia for more on this: https://en.wikipedia.org/wiki/Accelerating_expansion_of_the_universe

34. https://changingaging.org/aging101/gerotranscendence/

35. Psychologische Interpretation von Kinderträumen und älterer Literatur über Kinderträume. 2 Bände. Seminar von Prof. Dr. C.G. Jung Wintersemester 1938/39

36. *Coma: Key to Awakening* by Arnold Mindell, 1989.

37. According to Wikiquotes of the Tao Te Ching, "The Tao that can be told is not the eternal Tao; The name that can be named is not the eternal name." https://en.wikiquote.org/wiki/Tao

38. Daisetz Teitaro Suzuki, *Manual Of Zen Buddhism,* p. 80, http://www.buddhanet.net/pdf_file/manual_zen.pdf

39. See Wheeler's comments in chapter 36 of my *Quantum Mind, The Edge Between Physics and Psychology.*

40. https://www.newsweek.com/stephen-hawking-end-year-predictions-2017-755952

41. See the end of Chapter 2, figure 5

42. https://en.wikiquote.org/wiki/Laozi

43. https://spaceplace.nasa.gov/dark-matter/en/

Made in the USA
Monee, IL
22 May 2023

34271347R00164